"Finally, a book about how to handle the anger
This is a must-have book for teens, parents, and
anxiety. This book will connect the dots that are often missing when it comes to
anxiety-driven anger."

—**Natasha Daniels, LCSW**, anxiety and obsessive-compulsive disorder
(OCD) child therapist, creator of www.atparentingsurvival.com,
and author of *Anxiety Sucks*

"As a practicing psychologist working with teens for over twenty years, and as a
parent myself, I'm very excited to see Kelsey Torgerson Dunn's new book, *When
Anxiety Makes You Angry*, coming forward. With straightforward, engaging narra-
tive and many useful tools, strategies, and exercises, Torgerson Dunn's book offers
kids much-needed support in going beneath the surface of anger to the discomfort
and chaotic feel of underlying anxiety. Kids need to be seen for more than their
anger on the surface, and they need help like Torgerson Dunn's book in breaking
free of deeper anxiety so that anger is no longer necessary."

—**Mitch Abblett, PhD**, psychologist, and author of *Prizeworthy*

"Kelsey Torgerson Dunn's book on anxiety-driven anger for teens fills an important gap in skills-based learning, tapping into the intersection of two impactful
mind states in a uniquely nuanced way. As a clinician who encounters anger and
angst regularly in sessions, this book will be immensely useful in providing a thor-
ough and relatable framework for teens in and outside of the therapy experience!"

—**Katie Krimer, MA, LCSW**, therapist; authenticity coach;
author of *The Essential Self-Compassion Workbook for Teens*;
and founder of the wellness and self-growth platform, Growspace

"Kids need a much deeper understanding about the anxiety they experience, and to have the tools to both manage and prevent it. In her new book, *When Anxiety Makes You Angry*, Kelsey Torgerson Dunn lays out exactly what parents need to learn in order to best support their children to deal with their emotions."

> **—Tim Jordan, MD**, developmental and behavioral pediatrician, and author of *She Leads*

"*When Anxiety Makes You Angry* gives teens (and parents!) hope. Using exercises that build on one another, Kelsey Torgerson Dunn gently guides teens through the process of understanding their emotions and managing them well. No judgment or shame, just practical advice that can be used anywhere—even in the middle of a busy school day."

> **—Nicole Schwarz, LMFT**, parent coach, owner of Imperfect Families, and author of *It Starts with You*

"This book is an excellent contribution to the mental health resources available to teens and their parents at a time when they are so critically needed. The book is remarkably well written, jargon-free, and in an interesting and colorful style that will appeal to adolescents. The coping and problem-solving skills are evidence-based and introduced with real-life examples. Teens, parents, and teachers will find this creative and developmentally sensitive book highly informative."

> **—David A. Crenshaw, PhD, ABPP**, author; fellow of the American Psychological Association, Division of Child and Adolescent Psychology; and board-certified and licensed psychologist

"Finally, a resource for teens that struggle with anxiety that is masked by anger! Anger is an often-misunderstood symptom of anxiety leading to ineffective treatment choices and significant problems in teens' relationships with others. Kelsey Torgerson Dunn does a beautiful job of helping teens understand the fight response to anxiety, and skillfully guides them—step by step—in learning the choices in coping with these difficult emotions."

—**Angela Adamson Springer, LCSW**, owner of Calm Mind CBT, LLC in St. Louis, MO; and diplomate and certified trainer consultant of the Academy of Cognitive and Behavioral Therapies

# the *instant* help solutions series

Young people today need mental health resources more than ever. That's why New Harbinger created the **Instant Help Solutions Series** especially for teens. Written by leading psychologists, physicians, and professionals, these evidence-based self-help books offer practical tips and strategies for dealing with a variety of mental health issues and life challenges teens face, such as depression, anxiety, bullying, eating disorders, trauma, and self-esteem problems.

Studies have shown that young people who learn healthy coping skills early on are better able to navigate problems later in life. Engaging and easy-to-use, these books provide teens with the tools they need to thrive—at home, at school, and on into adulthood.

This series is part of the **New Harbinger Instant Help Books** imprint, founded by renowned child psychologist Lawrence Shapiro. For a complete list of books in this series, visit newharbinger.com.

# when anxiety makes you angry

## cbt anger management skills for teens with anxiety-driven anger

KELSEY TORGERSON DUNN, LCSW

Instant Help Books
An Imprint of New Harbinger Publications, Inc.

# Publisher's Note

*This publication is designed to provide accurate and authoritative information in regard to the subject matter covered. It is sold with the understanding that the publisher is not engaged in rendering psychological, financial, legal, or other professional services. If expert assistance or counseling is needed, the services of a competent professional should be sought.*

INSTANT HELP, the Clock Logo, and NEW HARBINGER are trademarks of New Harbinger Publications, Inc.

New Harbinger is an employee-owned company.

Distributed in Canada by Raincoast Books

Copyright © 2022 by Kelsey Torgerson Dunn
            Instant Help Books
            An imprint of New Harbinger Publications, Inc.
            5674 Shattuck Avenue
            Oakland, CA 94609
            www.newharbinger.com

Cover design by Amy Shoup

Acquired by Jennye Garibaldi

Edited by Karen Schader

All Rights Reserved

Library of Congress Cataloging-in-Publication Data on file

Printed in the United States of America

24     23     22

10   9   8   7   6   5   4   3   2   1          First Printing

*To Sofia, born during the pandemic. I love you forever.*

—Mama

# Contents

# Foreword

*"Hey Mallory, I'm writing a book about anxiety and anger, and I want you to write the foreword- will you do it?"*

When Kelsey first asked me this question my first response was, "Uh– Me? Really? Are you sure? Isn't there someone better?" To which she promptly replied, "Absolutely not! You're an expert when it comes to teen mental health, and I want you to do it."

Even though I'm a mental health therapist like Kelsey, and I have a YouTube library of 100 plus videos sharing how teens like you can improve their mental health, I also get anxious thoughts–much like the ones that probably inspired you to pick up this book and start reading. It's easy to go with our automatic negative thoughts as facts–even when they're mostly opinions.

You see, that's the thing about Kelsey–she's able to see the value in who you truly are–not all the noise and filters that surround your daily lives. And just like she did when she asked me to write the foreword for this book, she'll help you realize just how capable you are when it comes to managing your anxiety-driven anger for yourself with this book too.

Kelsey knows you're not meaning to be mean when you're feeling so much. When most people notice anger, they stop there and try to manage just that emotion. This book will help you investigate what's going on under that anger and what you can do about it. Like how the cognitive triangle in chapter 2 can help you reframe your experience. Or using emotions elevators from chapter 5 to help you know when and how to use your coping skills.

Each chapter is filled with funny, relatable examples–like the time your teacher called you out in an online classroom in front of everyone because your teacher didn't know how to DM you (big yikes!). Kelsey understands how these struggles impact teenagers in real ways that make sense.

Chapter 4 is my favorite because it focuses on how to find your explosion point, and Kelsey is not shy in letting you know that this stuff takes time. Everyone's starting point is a little bit different, so by taking the time to practice the exercises recommended in this chapter, you can start to recognize your window of tolerance and how you can plan for, and eventually open that window a bit wider over time.

My greatest advice for you as you start this book is to take breaks, go slow, and read it again later. With experience comes new knowledge, so revisiting the concepts in these chapters may take on new meaning once you start practicing what you learn. Kelsey even goes a step further than most authors and includes a nice breakdown of common scenarios that may pop up and which chapters make the most sense to revisit.

If you're brand new to these concepts, then you want to read this book in order because each chapter sets the foundation for the next chapter.

Remember that you don't have to be perfect as you read this book–therapists don't grade you. Being "good enough" is just fine with us!

I am so incredibly proud of my friend Kelsey for writing this book for you.

Though I'm even more proud of you for taking this step toward improving your mental health–you're pretty awesome!

With love and gratitude,

Mallory Grimste, LCSW

# Introduction for Parents

You're worried about your child. You love them, and you're worried about them. They're doing pretty well academically, you know they're smart, you know they're destined for greatness, and yet you're still anxious about them. They explode so easily. Every problem takes them from zero to sixty in mere seconds. They just seem so angry all the time, but even with the tantrums and the troubles, your gut is telling you something else is going on too.

You wonder what this might mean for them. You won't be there for them forever. What if they never tame their temper? What if they get in trouble with a professor at college? What if they explode at their boss when they're an adult? How will they make money? How will they find someone to love them the way they deserve? You know they're a good kid underneath it all, but what if nobody else can recognize that?

You have a teenager with something that looks like an explosive anger problem. They're moody. They're irritable. They're always on edge. You know that underneath all the prickliness, your sweet baby is still in there, but it is so hard for you to feel that tenderness when your teen is always pushing you away. You know at your core that something's wrong, and it probably feels like it's been wrong for a while.

Anger doesn't come out of nowhere, and it often masks a different underlying issue. Depression, grief, loss, ADHD, trauma—all these things that may be happening internally can lead to externalized anger, but the big one I want you to focus on is anxiety. Anxiety can look like anger, like stress, like perfectionism, and regardless of how it looks, it's getting in the way of everything else.

I'm Kelsey. I'm a licensed clinical social worker in Missouri, and I love to work with angry, anxious teens. As a therapist and anxiety specialist, I've worked with many, many families, and I tend to get two big questions from parents before our first session: "What's going on with my child?" and "Can you really help?"

When we think of how anxiety looks in kids and teens, we often think of those classic signs, like extreme anxiety around new people, test anxiety, or even panic attacks. When your child was younger, you may have seen some of these signs, like clinginess or being really upset when you'd drop them off at day care or school.

There's another side to anxious reactions too. This is what we're really talking about when we talk about the *fight-flight-or-freeze response*. Flight and freeze are on that classic anxiety side of reactions—like kids who want to run away on the first day of school or shut down and hide their face when you're introducing them to friends. Fight is equally valid, and yet we often miss this potential outcome when we're trying to diagnose anxiety. Because you're reading this book, your teen most likely has a lot more fight reactions than anything else. They get anxious or stressed, and their brain and body get primed to fight, stand their ground, and protect themself.

This book is organized the same way I structure ongoing therapy, where we learn skills one step at a time. Although we're not in therapy together, we're creating a solid foundation, one that your child can even build on if they decide to meet with a licensed therapist during or after this book. Your teen will learn how to identify what is going on underneath their anger. They'll build up an awareness of their thoughts, feelings, and behaviors (the foundation of *cognitive-behavioral therapy*) and break down the interaction between those three so that their anxiety-driven anger reactions aren't just operating on autopilot. They'll learn coping skills and ways to take the heat out of their anger and anxiety. They'll figure out how to problem solve without jumping to conclusions or getting so upset when you hold the line. They'll explore how to let go of things and move forward without ruminating, and they'll leave this book with a practical list of ways to strengthen these skills even further on their own or with the support of a therapist or counselor.

Being the parent of an angry teen can feel really lonely—especially when you know something more than just anger is going on. Focusing on those anger behaviors doesn't fix the root cause of what's really happening. Discipline and boundaries can get you only so far. Your friends, or your child's teachers, may be providing you advice on what to do and how to do it, and when nothing works, it's very disheartening. It's likely that you've already tried lots of different interventions. That's why it is so important to me that *When Anxiety Makes You Angry* is useful, practical, and something totally different from approaches you've tried before.

You want the best for your child. I'm going to be saying a lot of the same things that you've been saying; I'm just sharing the information in a different way, one that hopefully gets a little more investment and buy-in. As your teen reads this book, let them know that you're happy to talk through any of it with them, but you're going to leave it in their hands as much as they'd like. You're going to be working to foster their growth and emotional maturity by taking a more hands-off approach to this whole thing.

For parents who know their teens can't do it all alone, you can find resources, information, and strategies for you on my website, as well as a parent's guide, at, https://www.kelseytorgersondunn.com. In the meantime, hand this book over to your teen. Let them know you love them, and then we'll see what they do with it. You are a good parent. You are loving. You are supportive. You are helping your child. Thank you for letting me be a part of it.

# Introduction for Teens

Here we are, at the start of something big. Welcome! I'm glad you're here. I think this book is really going to help you. It's a book for anyone who knows they aren't angry, although everyone keeps telling them they are. It's for the teens who get in trouble all the time in class, for the graduating seniors who are freaked out about college, for the first-year high school students who are so overwhelmed about doing well that they snap at the smallest thing. It's a book for you, because you're here, you're reading this, and you want to get to work and feel better.

Right now, you're standing at the base of a mountain, looking at how high you'll have to climb. You've got your hiking shoes on. You brought your water bottle. You're feeling nervous. What if you don't make it? What if you only get halfway up, and that's as far as you can go?

Many people with anger problems are actually suffering from underlying anxiety, meaning they're trying to climb their mountain with only half the guidebook. The anger that seems so apparent from the outside is masking a lot of the fears, worries, and stresses that people have on the inside. When we just deal with what's going on externally, we miss the whole internal picture. Just trying to treat the behaviors that get you into trouble isn't enough. We need to dig in and figure out what's going on and why, so that you feel in charge of your reactions and emotions, instead of it being the other way around.

Think of this as your mountain climbing guidebook. You're going to get a trail map in here, you'll learn how to use new tools to climb better, and you'll have someone helping you find your own path—me!

I'm a therapist who loves working with anger, because I know the anger is not the full picture. In this book, I'm going to walk you through the exact outline I use in counseling with my clients, leaving you with a solid foundation to build on individually, with parental input, or even with your own therapist—whatever makes the most sense for you. You'll learn everything that is going on underneath your angry outbursts, so that you can figure out your triggers and choose a new way forward. You'll build skills to manage your thoughts, feelings, and behaviors so that you don't get so easily overwhelmed. You'll learn how to cope and how to solve problems and, most importantly of all, you'll learn how to move forward in your life by taming your internal anxiety and external anger.

When we're faced with a problem, we always have a choice. We can work it out or we can just move on. As you're standing here at the base of your mountain, looking at all the anger problems you've had in the past, feeling all the anxiety and stress that has been happening inside you, you might feel like just giving up. You might want to just sit down on the trail and not go any further. It's okay if you need to rest. You can decide how fast or how slow you want to climb that mountain, but no matter what, you have to move forward.

Honestly, there is a really hard trail in front of you. You can't just snap your fingers and get rid of all the difficult parts. But I know that other teens have climbed to the top, and I know you can too. Whenever you feel overwhelmed, stressed, or hopeless during the course of this book, take your time and take a deep breath, and then keep going. Deeply ingrained behaviors don't just solve themselves. They take work.

By the end of this book, you will have made some huge progress on this mountain. You're going to have this whole bag of tools you can use in your real life. You won't feel like your anger or stress or anxiety are as overwhelming as they were before. And even if those feelings do sometimes get overwhelming, you're going to know what to do about them. You'll experience a radical change. You'll learn how to deal with everything that doesn't go your way. I am so excited for you to begin this journey. Let's get started. You've got this.

# CHAPTER 1

# The Iceberg: What Else Is Underneath Your Anger?

When it comes to emotions, what you see isn't always what you get. We can look one way on the outside and be experiencing something totally different on the inside.

If you consistently get labeled as angry, this idea probably sounds pretty familiar to you. Teachers, parents, and even other kids at school may avoid you or say you have a temper. You may get in trouble for things that feel small to you, and even get blamed for things you don't think are your fault. This is frustrating, especially when it feels undeserved. While others may call you angry, aggressive, or mean, you probably haven't always identified that way. "I'm not angry," you think. "I'm just _____."

In this chapter, we want to fill in the blank. We want to dig into what else is going on, underneath what people have labeled as your anger problem. The first step to solving a problem is understanding it, and even if you're not 100 percent sure that you have an anger problem, you're probably pretty tired of people telling you that you do. Wouldn't it be nice to move past that and have people see you for who you really are? Let's figure out what's going on so that you know what to do about it; so that you can move forward, and everyone else can too.

# INSIDE/OUTSIDE ANGER (AND OTHER STUFF)

In my many years as a therapist, I've never worked with a teen who's *just* angry. There's usually something else going on, right underneath the surface. Getting labeled as angry comes down to how you express these other emotions and stressors. People might be reading into your external expressions of your internal emotions. You might have been thinking about the bad grade you just got on your test, and your teacher tells you to keep your temper in check. Or you're just focusing on your coach, and your teammate later asks why you seemed so upset. We're not always aware of what our body language is telling others.

There are two components to help us identify emotions: external clues and internal clues. External clues are how we look on the outside. People observe our facial expressions and body language, and from this data they decide how they think we're feeling. Internal clues are how we feel on the inside. These are the physiological components of emotions that we experience internally, but that others observing us wouldn't necessarily notice or correctly identify.

Since you're reading this book, my guess is that you express external anger clues that other people notice or make a big deal of. When you're upset, your body represents it in a certain way that an outside observer would code as an expression of anger. At a lower level of emotion, you might be crossing your arms, clenching your jaw, and rolling your eyes. At a higher level, you might add in yelling, forming your hands into fists, or even punching, kicking, and breaking things. If you observed someone with these external clues, you'd probably label that person as angry too.

The thing is, our external clues don't always match up to our internal experiences. Our internal clues may be telling a different story; one that we have to listen closely to in order to actually understand it.

## THE ANGER ICEBERG

The image of an iceberg is a helpful way to think about the relationship between your external expression of emotions and the internal feeling of them. If you've ever seen pictures of icebergs (or if you've ever seen them in person, which, hi, can I go on your next trip with you?) you know they look massive—and that's just the 10 percent above the water; the remaining 90 percent is down in the murky depths.

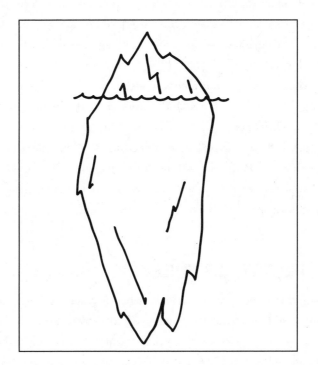

The tip of an anger iceberg represents your external clues, what people see when you're yelling or shouting or tensing your muscles. It's easy for someone to label you as angry since that's how you look. Because these clues are right on the surface, they're what most everyone pays attention to. Perhaps they're the only things you're really paying attention to right now, too, because those external behaviors are the ones getting you into trouble. But if you pay attention to only that 10 percent—to what you see on the surface—you're absolutely missing out on the bigger picture.

Maybe you've noticed that when people say you're angry, it doesn't really fit with what you're experiencing. Yes, you feel that frustration, but you feel a lot of other overwhelming things too. Maybe you notice some anger, but you also start to notice a lot of stress about doing well. Or you feel angry, and sad, and really nervous about whether or not people actually like you. Your parents may have anger issues that you've noticed your whole life, and you always feel like you need to be on edge too. Of course you're going to explode when something doesn't go your way.

These other co-occurring emotions—that stress, sadness, and nervousness—along with our background and history make up the hidden 90 percent of our iceberg. They're under the surface, meaning people often won't take the time to notice that you're experiencing something in addition to that anger you seem to be showing. Perhaps you're not fully aware of these emotions underneath the surface either. It takes work to dive deeper, rather than just accepting what's going on at surface level.

## FIGHT, FLIGHT, OR FREEZE

To understand your personal experience when it comes to anger and all the overwhelming stuff underneath it, we need to explore how our bodies and brains prime us for dangerous situations. Many of us have heard of the fight-or-flight response. There's a third option, freeze, that explains how people may react during an overwhelmingly stressful situation. These healthy automatic reactions occur before we can even really stop and think about what's going on.

Here's how it works: Let's say you're walking in the woods, and you come across a bear. You almost sense it before you even see it, noticing a slight prickling along your neck, and suddenly, that big brown bear is right in front of you.

Your brain feels like it doesn't have time to think; it just needs you to *react*! And quickly!

Immediately, your brain tells your body to release stress hormones. Your body floods with adrenaline and cortisol. Your muscles tense, your heart rate increases, and your breathing feels fast and short. Your brain tells you that you have three options and no time to think about them. You can

*fight* that bear,

take *flight*, running from the bear as fast as you can,

or

*freeze* and play dead.

Okay—yikes! Stressful! Let's take a step back—thankfully, you're not in the woods with a bear. Looking at these automatic responses, you can probably understand the survival instinct running underneath. Rationally, though, these options that our brain throws out may not be the best choice. Can you really take on a bear in fist-to-fist combat? Or run away from the bear when the woods are covered in mud and you don't actually know where you are? This is the main problem with our fight-flight-or-freeze reaction. We don't have the time to think through the pros and cons of what we're doing. Our stress response has taken control of the wheel.

To take this a step further, a lot of the time our brains activate the fight-flight-or-freeze response even when we're not in a life-or-death situation. That same part of your brain that says, "It's a bear, danger!" is also telling you, "Dad seems mad, danger!" or "That kid looked at me weird, he must be talking about me, danger!" Your brain is just trying to protect you, but it's getting in the way of you really thinking through what's going on.

People often get labeled as angry because they tend to respond to stressful, overwhelming, or fearful situations with a *fight* response. That fight response is just as valid as flight or freeze, but it's often the response that gets us in the most trouble. We get into a stressful situation, and we yell or shout or scream because, underneath it all, our brain is telling us that we're in danger and we have to defend ourselves. This is normal, healthy, and from a biological perspective, understandable. But it doesn't mean that people are going to like that you're doing it.

The goal is to retrain our brains and build up impulse-control skills so that we're not reacting so automatically. Let's check in below and see which response your brain normally selects: fight, flight, or freeze. Knowing this will help a lot when it comes to figuring out your next step: What do you do about it?

## Fight-Flight-or-Freeze Check-In

How would you be most likely to react in each of these situations?

You're at the end of the lunch line and waiting to pay. A kid bumps into you, and you drop most of the food from your tray. It seems like people are laughing. Do you

*Fight:* Push the kid back and tell him that if he does it again, you're happy to take it outside?

Take *flight:* Drop the rest of the tray, leave the lunch line immediately (because people are *obviously* laughing at you), and go hide out in the bathroom?

*Freeze:* Stay in line, not knowing what to do next, until a staff member comes over to ask what's wrong?

You're in your bedroom doing your homework. You get to a ridiculously hard math equation that you have no idea how to solve. Do you

*Fight:* Start breaking pencils, toss your books to the ground, and yell (so loudly that your mom comes in to check on you), "This is freaking impossible!!!"?

Take *flight*: Feel so overwhelmed that you have to get out of your room ASAP, and run outside to your car to just drive away and get some space?

*Freeze*: Stare at the problem until you realize you've been looking at it for over an hour and haven't done any other work?

You almost always do your chores, but tonight your dad is really getting on your case about emptying the dishwasher. You're planning to finish up an episode on TV first, but he comes in, turns off the TV, and says you're obviously not listening. He's grounding you. Do you

*Fight*: Shout, "That's so unfair! Why don't you ever give me time to relax before you make me do all your stupid chores?"

Take *flight*: Leave the room as fast as you can because you're afraid you're going to freak out?

*Freeze*: Totally shut down and ignore him until he goes away?

It's finals week. You're teetering right between a B+ and an A- in Spanish class, and you really want a good grade since you'll be applying to college next year. You've reached the portion of the test where you're supposed to have a one-on-one conversation with your teacher, fully in Spanish. After your first few sentences, she jumps in and says, "Let's start again. You're making a lot of small mistakes already." Do you

*Fight*: Blurt out, "Why are you being such a jerk?" and feel the impulse to rip up all your notes for the test?

Take *flight*: Feel a panic attack starting up, and say you need to use the restroom ASAP?

*Freeze*: Go totally blank. Your words can't even come out anymore because you're afraid you've already ruined everything?

You're at your school's homecoming dance. You were supposed to meet your friends here, and then they text the group chat to say they're out getting ice cream first. They don't invite you. It seems like everyone at the dance is watching you while you're just standing by yourself. Do you

*Fight:* Text them back to say they're being so rude that you don't even want to be friends with them anymore?

Take *flight:* Call your mom and tell her she needs to pick you up *now*, and start walking home before she's even on her way?

*Freeze:* Watch everyone watching you, stay in this one spot with your heart pounding, and feel tears welling up in your eyes?

You may have different responses in different situations. Ask yourself, is there one that you use more often than the others? Do you notice any patterns? If you do, how do you feel about having these responses? What would you like to change?

There are no wrong answers. The first step to solving any problem is identifying it. We want to build up your understanding of yourself and your reactions.

## OUR FEELINGS, OURSELVES

Underneath all these reactions is a sense of danger that makes us feel anxious, but we don't always catch that feeling. Much like we all have an idea of how anger is supposed to look on the outside, we also have a pretty good idea of what we expect anxiety to look like.

I like to call these expected anxious reactions "classic" anxiety, meaning your typical outside observer will quickly identify that you are experiencing anxiety. It's easy to empathize with these classic signs. You know what they look like and what to expect, and so you feel compassion for the person going through them. You see flight or freeze, and you get what they're going through.

The other side of anxiety, fight, is not as expected. It's harder to empathize with anxiety that looks more like an anger response. We don't like when people are angry, and we expect people to control their anger. But what about when their anger is hard to control? What about when that anger is actually due to anxiety?

There are a lot of different types of anxiety, but let's look at the top three that I've worked with in my practice, and talk through what people might expect to see versus how it looks through that fight-reaction lens.

## Generalized Anxiety Disorder (GAD)

Generalized Anxiety Disorder (GAD) is one of the most common types of anxiety. It describes a general feeling of nervousness, anxiety, and stress, experienced in a variety of situations. In the "classic" sense, people would expect to see you feeling nervous in a variety of situations, disengaging from others, avoiding situations, or even demonstrating some perfectionism because your general anxiety makes you worried about being perceived as a failure. Now through that fight lens, you would still be experiencing all that internal nervousness, anxiety, and stress, but that increase would cause you to be more prone to temper tantrums and blowing up. The perfectionism that people might expect would instead look like you being really controlling. The root is the same, but the appearance is different. A fun fact (or at least a fun fact for me as a therapist who loves anxiety-driven anger!) is that anger and irritability are actually symptoms of GAD in the *DSM-5* (the American Psychiatric Association's diagnostic and statistical manual)! So even though it's in the manual that therapists use to make diagnoses, therapists can miss it, and think that something else must be causing the anger.

## Social Anxiety Disorder

Social anxiety disorder is a fear of new people, social situations, and judgment from others. This fear of judgment leads people with social anxiety disorder to avoid social settings. On the classic side, people with social anxiety are expected to be really shy, avoid interactions, and of course have trouble with public speaking. On that fight-reaction side, fearing judgment from others may make you judge others first. Why let other people be mean to you when you could just be mean to them? This fight version of social anxiety may also lead people to ask themselves, "Why should I care if they don't like me? I disliked them first."

## Panic Disorder

People with panic disorder experience multiple panic attacks. A panic attack makes you feel like your heart is stopping, you can't breathe, and maybe even are going to die. People expect a classic panic attack to be very apparent from the outside. But actually, people can experience internal panic attacks without really showing others, and instead of looking overwhelmed and frightened, they seem totally fine on the outside—which makes it even more surprising when they yell at someone, "Leave me alone!" "Give me some space!" or "Stay away from me!" It may not seem to an outside observer that the yelling is due to anxiety, but it is.

# BODY CLUES ACTIVITY

Most of us are so used to paying attention to what's happening on the outside that we don't always take the time to think through what's going on inside. You might not know if anxiety is underneath your emotional outbursts either. We need to dive deeper and explore what your internal emotional experience is telling you. What's happening in your brain? What's happening in your body? These are the crucial questions to help us broaden our understanding of ourselves, so that we can actually figure out what's going on instead of just feeling like we explode all the time.

Everyone experiences feelings a bit differently. There are some expected physiological reactions, but I want you to get really clear about your own individual experience. Until you learn how to really clue in and listen to your emotions, we won't have the best plan to deal with them. Now let's get to work.

If you're artistically inclined, pull out a piece of paper, get a few colored pencils or pastels, and start drawing an outline of your body. I usually stick with something basic: a circle head, a couple of big arms, a torso, and some legs. If you'd like a downloadable version of this, you can find the link on our resources page at the back of the book—plus lots of other materials that will crop up over these next chapters. Don't get caught up in making this look perfect—it's just for you. You're also welcome to journal, jotting down your ideas as you consider the prompts that follow.

First, think about the last time you felt angry. Really bring the details into this situation. Think about your five Ws: Who was there? What happened? Where was this? When did it occur? Why do you think this happened? And why do you think it made you so angry?

When you've found that angry feeling, notice where you experience it in your body. If you're using your body outline, color in those areas with a color that really represents anger for you. If you're journaling, note where you experience this and how it feels. Do you notice tightness anywhere? Does your heart beat faster? Slower? Maybe your breathing picks up or even feels like it stops. Note any places that seem hot or cold, and any reactions your body wants to have—kicking, punching, ripping. Where are those reactions being held in your body? Does that impulse to kick something start mostly in your foot, or your leg, or do you really just feel it in your heart? Make sure you mark down every place you feel it in your body, even if it's a small part of the bigger picture.

Next, let's think about the last time you felt anxious. Maybe it was before a test, or walking into a party, or coming home when you just knew that you were going to be in trouble. Once you've found that feeling, do the same thing. Color where you notice it on your body with a color that represents anxiety for you, or write down where you experience that feeling in your body. Note the physical sensation of that feeling.

When I get anxious, I notice that my heart beats a little faster, my breathing becomes shallow, and I almost feel sick to my stomach. If I'm especially nervous, I might also get sweaty palms. Remember, emotions are individualized experiences, so you may notice nervousness in the same cluster that I do, or you may experience it in other areas of your body.

You may notice an overlap between where you experience anger and where you experience anxiety. It's okay if you don't, but for many, this anxiety and anger overlap is super common, and it's the main reason it's so easy for our wires to get crossed about what emotions are actually underneath our outburst.

Now let's look at stress, which can be a third factor in this anxiety and anger relationship. For some, stress and anxiety feel the same, and for others it's a little different. What does stress feel like for you, and how do you know you're stressed rather than anxious? No matter how you experience it, pick out a stress color or pick up your pen, and identify where that feeling is in your body. What's the physical experience? What urges do you notice in your body? How can you tell that you're stressed and not something else?

Looking at your picture now, does your experience of stress overlap with your anxiety and with your anger? What feels the same? What parts of your body get activated by all three?

Feel free to continue this exercise with other emotions as more feelings come to mind. Some other important emotions to explore and identify are sadness, grief, boredom, and happiness, and you're welcome to dig further as you broaden your emotional repertoire.

Let's take a step back and observe. Ask yourself:

- What do you notice about your picture or your journaling?

- What emotions seem to overlap?

- What emotions seem to have similar physiological responses for you?

- Where do you notice anger and anxiety emotions clustering or starting in your body?

- How can this activity provide information for your future anger and anxiety management plan?

As you dive into your picture or writing, you may notice certain patterns emerge. Many people notice an increase in heart rate, shallowness of breath, and increase in muscle tension for anger, anxiety, and stress. Because we're experiencing the same type of reaction for three different emotions, our brain can have trouble sorting out how we actually feel.

This is also why, hello, I've written this book *for you*, the angry teen who is actually probably pretty anxious too. Your anger and your anxiety can fuel your body into reacting in ways you don't really like, especially when that anxiety and stress and anger reach overwhelming proportions.

## ANXIETY-DRIVEN ANGER

Sometimes when we feel angry, we feel anxious as well. We can feel anxiety about how we're going to respond, how the other person is going to react, or the potential negative consequences of our anger-driven actions. Anger and anxiety can feed off one another, and the heightening of one can lead to the heightening of the other.

Consider the last time you had a big school project. You may have felt anxious about finishing it and getting a good grade. Perhaps you just had a few more pieces to put together the night before it was due. Imagine that at this moment, when you're feeling a lot of anxiety about completing the assignment, your mom comes in to tell you that you forgot to take out the trash.

Normally, taking out the trash is a small inconvenience and a minor stressor. This time, because of the anxiety you're already feeling about the school project, you just explode. You start yelling at your mom—who probably doesn't deserve it, even if it feels like she does in the moment. That anxiety you were experiencing about school increased your stress level, and that extra stressor of your mom's reminder led to you reaching your explosive tipping point. Your mom is going to label your reaction as angry. You yelled at her! That's so disrespectful! How could you?! But we really know that it wasn't just anger. It was anxiety about school that led to this huge reaction.

Anger and anxiety lead to a few expected physical responses for most everyone. With anger, your brain sends information to a few key areas in your body. Your muscles tense. You feel a burst of energy. Your heart rate increases as more blood pumps through your body. Your breathing rate typically increases, in order to get more oxygen to your muscles. Your attention narrows, making your brain feel super focused on whatever is causing your anger, or making your mind feel like it's totally blank.

It may surprise you, but anxiety creates the exact same heart-pumping, muscle-tensing, breath-quickening, attention-narrowing reactions. If your body is doing the same type of thing when you're angry and when you're anxious, doesn't it make sense that your brain might get confused about interpreting how you're feeling?

You, of course, feel both anger and anxiety. Sometimes, though, your brain gets confused about what emotion is happening. When it gets used to interpreting reactions in a certain way, you end up having to retrain your brain to stop and think, and figure out what is actually going on with your emotions.

Your brain is connected by millions of neurons, with electrical currents passing through them at lightning-fast speed. Neural pathways that we use again and again get strengthened. It's like a ravine that's been carved through stone over millennia. Even the Grand Canyon started as flat land with a river running through it. As the water continued to flow along that one path, the land was carved out more and more. Your emotional reactions work the same way. When your brain gets so used to taking in one piece of information and choosing one response to that info, your reactions become second nature.

You're not always in charge of what happens to you. Your teacher corrects you in front of the whole class, your mom makes you do chores when you have a huge essay due, or your friends all decide to hang out without you. These things happen outside your control, and they're upsetting.

What we *are* in charge of is how we feel and how we react. If your brain always interprets your emotional response to these stressors as anger, or other people in your life are always telling you that you seem so mad, you go through life assuming that's it.

Sometimes we're mad. Sometimes we're stressed, but it looks like we're mad. Sometimes we're anxious, but our brains think we're mad. Sometimes we're mad and anxious and overwhelmed all at the same time. It's important to take a pause and figure out what emotions are coming up for you, instead of just assuming it's the thing you always feel.

It doesn't often seem like it, but we're in charge of our emotions, not the other way around. We get to decide how we feel. We get to decide how we react. And we get to decide how to move forward when stuff doesn't go the way we want. We can respond to the fallout from our reactions and choose a different response for next time.

# CHAPTER 2

# The Cognitive Triangle

Do you ever just feel totally overwhelmed out of nowhere? I remember walking to class one morning in my first semester of college. I felt this huge wave of anxiety. There was nothing I could point to that was making me feel that way. Nothing I was nervous about and no big deadlines or uncomfortable interactions on the docket. If anything, it was supposed to be a great day. The weather was beautiful. I was so happy to be on campus and really felt like I was growing into the independent person I'd always wanted to be. On that day, I had a full schedule of classes that I loved. But something was going on, and I didn't know what. The uncertainty put me on edge.

As the day continued, I was able to focus on my lectures and positive interactions with friends. That nameless anxiety retreated to the background; yet whenever I remembered the feeling, it came back. I would notice my toes curling up, my shoulders tensing, my jaw clenching.

I found myself becoming more abrupt during conversations, and more easily frustrated by small inconveniences. The line for the salad bar was long, and I rolled my eyes at the person taking her time to pick out each individual cherry tomato she wanted. What was her deal? My friend complained about this guy she had a crush on. I told her she needed to get over him because he wasn't that great anyway. My professor forgot handouts, and I silently fumed at the lack of consideration. So unprofessional! I didn't mean to be mean, and I didn't like noticing my temper—but it kept happening.

We can't always figure out why we're feeling what we're feeling. We snap at our parents for no real reason, or our hands start to sweat on the way to a friend's house even though we're excited to go. Stressors can build up in the background. Even if we can't point to the exact cause of an emotion, our brain and our body are constantly in communication with one another, sometimes at a subconscious level. We're not always able to translate what's happening to our internal selves. That's what we need to do, though, to help with anxiety-driven anger. We need to start speaking our body's language so we really know what's going on and how it is impacting us.

This language is especially important to be aware of when it comes to crossing our anxiety and anger wires. Just like on my anxious, angry day in college, your body can be experiencing physical anxiety, and your brain interprets it as anger. Or you tell yourself that you're feeling overwhelmed and can't handle one more responsibility, and your body readies itself for a huge outburst, just in case. Your body is primed by your thoughts, and vice versa.

That particular day in college, I couldn't point to a reason to feel anxious, but I could point to lots of reasons to feel annoyed. Looking at it now, it's clear that my nameless anxiety directly impacted my temper that day. Waking up anxious made my brain think something bad was going to happen. My body reacted by being on guard, and then my brain confused that anxiety and guardedness with anger and frustration. If I had been able to recognize this, I could have been more mindful of my unkind reactions and felt calmer about the small annoyances that occurred.

There's a crucial link between our thoughts, our feelings, and our behaviors. It's not always easy to figure out why you're feeling what you're feeling, but it's so important to pay attention to what's going on between these three key pieces. By knowing what we're feeling and thinking, and why we're acting the way that we're acting, we can make choices about what we do—instead of just feeling like things are happening to us. Knowledge is power.

## THOUGHTS, FEELINGS, AND BEHAVIORS: GETTING THE DETAILS

Thoughts, feelings, and behaviors all feed into one another, and the relationship between them is the foundation of a type of evidence-based therapy called cognitive behavioral therapy (CBT). Cognitive = cognitions, aka thoughts, or what we tell ourselves in our brains; behavioral = behaviors, of course; and therapy is the process by which we untangle, understand, and impact the Cs and the Bs. CBT is all about the interactions between what you're telling yourself and how you're reacting. It has a ton of research behind it and is proven to be effective at reducing those overwhelming moments of anger and anxiety.

These thoughts, feelings, and behaviors all impact one another. This relationship provides a helpful framework for figuring out what's going on with you and why. Obviously, when you're in the middle of an overwhelming experience, it's difficult to take a step back and ask yourself, "Hmm, I wonder what thought is going on in my head right now?" I'd love for you to get to that point eventually! But for right now, let's use these three components to explore what's happening, why, and what you can change.

## FACT OR OPINION?

Sometimes our brains come up with thoughts that sound true at first but, upon further reflection, turn out not to be. It's like the difference between a fact and an opinion. A fact is 100 percent true and provable through evidence, and an opinion is an interpretation of what's going on.

I am absolutely in love with snickerdoodles. They've been my 100 percent all-time favorite cookie for as long as I can remember. If I were to say, "Snickerdoodles use cream of tartar to make them slightly acidic," that's a fact. You can look up multiple recipes online, find the scientific evidence behind cream of tartar as a slightly acidic leavening agent, and read tons of sources to back up this claim.

"Snickerdoodles are typically rolled in cinnamon and sugar" is a provable fact, as is, "Snickerdoodles are round and have a crackly crust." Not only can we read about this, we can see it with our own eyes. We have evidence.

Now if I were to say, "Snickerdoodles are a superior cookie," or "People who like snickerdoodles are better than people who prefer chocolate chip cookies, because chocolate chip cookies are so boring," these statements are obviously opinions. Of course, I can still back up these opinions with evidence to support my claims. I could share that my grandmother also loves snickerdoodles more than any other cookie, and she has eighty years of cookie expertise to back up her preference. I could point out that the cream of tartar in the recipe is a unique ingredient and the sourness it provides makes snickerdoodles superior. Again, there's evidence here to back up my opinion, but that evidence doesn't prove that my opinion is true. Someone could just as easily come along and dispute my claims, using different provable pieces of evidence to support their beliefs. The facts are true. The interpretation is what's open to debate.

It gets tricky when you're used to listening only to your opinion, and the first opinion that comes to your mind. You might not realize that you're just hearing your interpretation of the facts. Instead, your brain is certain that you are thinking about what's really going on, with totally unbiased clarity. We can be very focused on what we *know* to be true, even if it's actually just our opinion. Importantly, this happens in our own minds, meaning we don't receive anyone else's input unless we're sharing our thoughts with others.

Let's say your friends didn't invite you to go to the movies with them, and your brain tells you that they absolutely, positively must hate you. They didn't invite you, so this must be true. Or your brother takes your iPad and "accidentally" breaks it, and your dad says it was a mistake and you need to get over it. Obviously, your dad must love your brother more than you to take his side.

It's easy to jump to an explanation and convince yourself that it's the truth. You end up telling yourself that it's a fact that your friends hate you, or it's a fact that you're not your father's favorite. But are these really facts?

Your thoughts may look angry at first glance, but if we take a step back, we can notice an underlying current of insecurity there too. You're mad at your friends for excluding you, and at the same time you're worried they don't like you anymore. You're frustrated with your dad for taking your brother's side, and simultaneously feeling anxious about your relationship with him compared to his relationship with your brother. Take special note of this double whammy. Those emotions, especially when combined, can cloud your judgment.

There's always another way to interpret the data. Your brain may even quietly be coming up with a calmer explanation before that loud, anxious, angry voice takes over. The first step to giving this quiet voice more space is to recognize when those automatic assumptions are just opinions. Yes, of course, your father could really have a favorite, or maybe your friends really didn't invite you because they hate you. This could be true. But what if there's something else going on?

## COGNITIVE TRIANGLE WALK-THROUGH AND REFRAME

What you tell yourself influences how you feel, and how you feel affects how you react. When you believe your opinions are facts, your opinions will impact both your emotions and your behaviors. The connection between thoughts, feelings, and behaviors is easy to explore using the cognitive triangle.

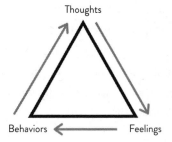

At the top of the triangle, we have our *thoughts*, or what we're telling ourselves in our brain. Let's say you walk into the school's library. One student in a group of seniors makes eye contact with you, and then the whole table starts quietly laughing with one another. What's the first thought that might pop into your head?

If you're like most people, you might notice a thought like, "They must be laughing at me." Let's travel down that triangle and check in with your *feelings*. If your thought is, "They must be laughing at me," what emotion do you notice coming up for you? Often, that thought might bring up some anger and frustration, or even a bit of fear and embarrassment.

We'll move over to that third corner of the triangle, your *behaviors*. You walk into the library. A group of seniors starts laughing. You tell yourself they're laughing at you. You feel frustrated and anxious. Do you walk up to them and yell, "Stop laughing at me!"? Do you complain to the librarian about how disrespectful they are? Do you slam your books down and glare at them? What would be your go-to behavior in this sort of situation?

Walking through this cognitive triangle, you might feel pretty justified in your reaction. Your brain says they're obviously laughing at you. Of course you're upset, and of course you want to react in a way to get them to stop. But what if your first thought isn't actually correct? What if there's something else going on?

Instead of jumping to the conclusion that they're laughing at you, try coming up with something else to tell yourself. What if they're laughing about a joke totally unrelated to you? What if they're talking about a teacher? What if one of them is your brother's friend, and she was just talking about him when you walked in? Unless you 100 percent know for sure that they were laughing at you, any of these explanations could be possible. Some may be more likely than others, but you get to decide what thought will best help you impact your feelings and behaviors for the better.

Let's go through the cognitive triangle again, using a more helpful thought to reframe our perspective. Instead of telling yourself that they are laughing at you, you say, "They're probably laughing about something that has nothing to do with me." Rather than feeling frustrated, you may feel curious, or you may just feel calm and uninterested. And then, instead of slamming your books on the table and glaring at them—an immediate, big reaction that you probably would regret after the fact—you quietly get to work.

What changed? Both times, a table full of seniors laughed at the same time you walked into the library. In one scenario, you react aggressively. In the other, you go about your day and get some work done. As you can see, the situation starts the same. What changed is what you told yourself about what happened, and that impacted how you felt and what you did.

Taking the time to stop and think through the cognitive triangle can have important impacts. Not only do you give yourself the space to examine your automatic assumptions, you also directly influence your reactions. Often, the teens with the big reactions feel embarrassed about their loss of control, even if they feel justified in being so upset.

There can be some negative consequences to that immediate anxiety-driven anger outburst. You might get in trouble for your reactions, sure, but you might also feel shame and guilt. You might directly impact your social standing at the school after a blowup, or you might just be worried that you did, which then leads to a whole other set of automatic thoughts, fears, and unhelpful interpretations of what's going on. There's a chain reaction of thought, feeling, behavior, and consequence that reverberates down your whole day. It can feel automatic, and like you're stuck in this pattern. But you're not. You have the power to change this.

Who is in charge of your reactions, and your feelings, and your thoughts?

You are.

## CBT SCENARIOS

Divide a piece of paper into two columns and draw two rows of triangles in each. You'll use the first row for this sample scenario, and then you'll continue with your own example.

Sample scenario:

You and your younger sister get into a fight about who gets to control the remote and pick the next TV show. She calls you a jerk. You throw the remote across the room. Your mom comes down and tells you to stop it. You don't, and you end up slapping your sister's arm. You get grounded, so now you can't hang out with your friends and have to stay at home all weekend. Your sister isn't punished at all.

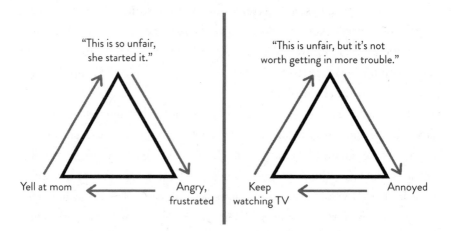

Using your first cognitive triangle, write down (1) the first thought that would pop into your mind if this situation actually happened to you, (2) what emotion that thought leads to, and (3) what behavior that emotion would bring up.

In the second column on the same row, let's go through the reframe. What else could you tell yourself during this situation? What feeling does that thought lead to? And what behavior results?

Now it's your turn. Identify two situations from your own life that didn't really go the way you wanted. These can be recent, or events that happened a while ago that still stick with you. For each situation, complete your cognitive triangle: thought, emotion, and behavioral reaction. Then, work through the triangle in the next column using a cognitive reframe. What else could you tell yourself? What emotion follows that thought? What behavior comes after that feeling?

After you finish your two situations and two reframes, let's sit with this a bit. I want you to take a minute with your paper and write down what you notice. What consequences, internally or externally, happened in these situations? How would those consequences have changed if you had listened to your reframed thought instead? How do you feel when you look at these cognitive triangles? What do they tell you about yourself?

Also ask yourself if these situations point to a larger pattern for you. Were these just one-off situations, or do these types of problems often come up? Are you usually pretty pleased about how you respond to stressors, or do you often wish, upon reflection, that you had done something differently?

People can look at their cognitive triangles and come up with some pretty negative self-talk. They tell themselves that they're bad people, or that their brains are broken. I don't know if this is coming up for you, but it's okay if it is. These are just thoughts too.

Let's go through some thoughts that *might* be coming up for you about yourself following this cognitive triangle exercise, and get you to a more helpful headspace for moving forward.

*My brain is messed up because it always comes up with bad thoughts. I always tell myself something negative.*

There's actually no such thing as a bad thought! People often call thoughts bad when they really just mean that a thought isn't so helpful. We'll talk through this more in Chapter 3, but I want to assure you there's nothing wrong with having these thoughts pop up. They're very understandable, natural, and even healthy. Your brain is working to keep you safe, even when it's being self-critical. We just have to coach it to take a step back and come up with some more helpful thoughts instead. Reframe this thought to something like, "My brain often comes up with unhelpful thoughts. This is something my brain does to try and protect me. I don't always like it, but it is what it is—and I'm reading this book to try and make it better."

*I have an anger problem. Maybe that makes me a bad person.*

Yeah, that's true, you might have a problem with your anger. Your anger feels like it gets too big too quickly. Your anger gets in the way of you calming down and moving forward from your problems. Your anger may seem embarrassing when it leads to an outburst. The thing is, pure anger is a really important emotion to feel because it lets us know we don't like what's going on. Also, from Chapter 1, you know that your anger is often just the tip of the iceberg and covering up some underlying anxiety. Does feeling anger or anxiety make you a bad person? Of course not. Can you still feel like you have trouble with anger and anxiety, even if you're not a bad person? Yes! We can work on your anger and anxiety, but telling yourself that you're a bad person is only going to make it harder, and it's not even true. Be kind to yourself. Try, "Anger can sometimes get me in trouble," rather than "I have an anger problem."

*I'm hopeless, and even if I try and work on this, it's never going to change.*

Listen. I absolutely empathize with you. It's a lot of work to change, but that doesn't make you hopeless. Change doesn't happen all at once. Instead, each positive change you make is like reaching another rung up the ladder to where you want to be. Keep a picture in your mind of how you would like to be different. Recognize that working through each chapter of this book is another step in that direction. Replace your hopeless thought with, "I can make small changes. I can grow. I know that feeling hopeless is normal, and at the same time, I'm not hopeless. I'm motivated."

Any other thoughts that you notice? Concerns you feel? Worries you have? Remember, any thought is just a thought! It's not necessarily true, and if it's not helpful, you don't have to listen to it.

# WHAT ELSE CAN WE CHANGE?

The really cool thing about the cognitive triangle is that we can change our thoughts, but we can also change our feelings and behaviors, and have an impact on the overall outcome of that situation. Above, we explored how to flip our thoughts to something more helpful, but we can also figure out ways to cool down our emotions, and we can choose different behaviors in the moment. Cooling down our emotions and using different behaviors will change our thoughts too. It's pretty nifty.

## Changing Our Feelings

Let's say you're in a situation where your friend blames you for spreading a rumor, and you had nothing to do with it. You tell yourself, "I can't believe this!

And she doesn't believe me! There's nothing I can say!" The situation brings up painful memories of times when your friends excluded you in the past. You're feeling defensive and nervous, and even a little frustrated about what's going on. You start hyperventilating. At a certain point, your emotions get too overwhelming for you to even think clearly.

In this type of situation, it's going to be really hard to flip your thoughts first because of your strong emotions and your pattern of behavior. Your brain is used to thinking a particular way, and those heightened emotions get in the way of clear thoughts.

What we need to do is work on lowering your emotions through some kind of relaxation activity, like the tools we'll cover in depth in Chapter 5. We need to take the heat out of what you're feeling. Cooling down your emotional level is impactful because it helps lower the temperature of the whole situation, so that you're not automatically flowing into those typical behaviors and responses that so often get you in trouble.

As you calm down, your brain has an easier time of matching that calmness with a calm thought. You've relaxed enough to be able to tell yourself, "This is not a great situation, but I understand why my friend's upset. Maybe I can help them figure out what to do next. At the very least, I can empathize and let them know I'm on their side." You decide to talk with them. They're able to calm down too. You two move forward and solve the problem, and you're back on the same team.

The flip side of this relationship is that feeling anxious or angry means that you're more prone to have follow-up anxious or angry thoughts, and subsequent anxious or angry behaviors. Remember that anxious day in college I described at the start of this chapter? I couldn't really point to any particular thoughts that made me feel anxious that morning. Instead, that anxiety-driven anger just started as a feeling, and it led to more angry behaviors and more angry thoughts. If I had been able to calm down that feeling, my body would have been less tense, and I would have had an easier time coming up with more helpful, less frustrated thoughts. I wouldn't have been as likely to snap at my friend, roll my eyes at the girl picking out her tomatoes, and get mad at my teacher for forgetting the handouts. Calming down at the start, and dealing with that nameless anxiety, would have had a hugely positive impact. Changing the feeling would have helpfully reverberated down the rest of my day.

## Changing Our Behaviors

Calming down obviously makes it easier to choose calmer thoughts and demonstrate calmer behaviors. Another way to recircuit your brain and impact that cognitive triangle is to get outside of your norm.

Our brain is constantly forming and rewiring connections; this ability to change neural pathways is called *neuroplasticity*. Instead of using the same behavior over and over again, if we change how we normally react to situations, we can positively impact our thoughts and feelings.

Let's say you're feeling really depressed. Normally, you stay in your room and isolate, but the more you isolate, the more depressed you feel. If you choose a totally different behavior instead, like going for a walk outside, getting active, or using another coping skill, you get out of the rut. Your behavior changes your feeling, and it changes your subsequent thoughts. By focusing on the action part of your triangle, you feel less down, and you end up telling yourself more helpful things.

Or let's say when you feel really angry, you normally punch a pillow. If you choose a totally different behavior, like hugging that pillow instead, you're doing something outside of your norm, which helps open your brain up to subsequent new feelings and new thoughts. Choosing different reactions than your brain would normally expect helps it take a step back. You get out of that set stimulus response.

During my anxious, angry day at school, I could have impacted my cognitive triangle by engaging in actions that helped me feel better. For example, I love doing yoga, so maybe I could have noticed that anxiety and fit in time to take a yoga class. Those calm movements would have helped regulate my emotions, and I would have been in a gentler headspace, making me less likely to get upset with the small stresses that happened over the course of my day.

It was really nice outside on that anxious, angry day. On that behavioral corner, I also could have chosen to sit outside in the sun, catching some rays and getting some vitamin D. Just choosing to be outside and taking a break would have helped. I would have felt calmer. I would have been able to tell myself calmer thoughts.

## YOUR BRAIN ON CBT

Hopefully, you can now see that CBT, and specifically your knowledge of the cognitive triangle, can change how you think, feel, and react to a vast number of different situations. In addition to just seeming helpful, CBT can actually change your brain. When you are a person with anxiety, your brain has really high reactivity in your *amygdala*, which is the part of your brain leading your fight-flight-or-freeze response. Researchers found that patients with social anxiety disorder who completed CBT treatment had less reaction in their amygdala after treatment. CBT not only helped their social anxiety symptoms diminish, it also structurally changed their brains (Månsson et al 2016).

Becoming consciously aware of your thoughts, feelings, and behaviors, and choosing to change them, helps your brain. You'll see a positive impact over time when you're regularly interrupting your unhelpful thoughts and choosing more helpful ones. You'll feel less reactivity to situations when you recognize that your emotions are heightened and choose to lower them. You'll be less embarrassed or regretful about your reactions when you're consciously choosing to respond to stressors in a calmer way. This is all true. And you're changing your brain! That's pretty amazing.

# NOW WHAT?

Learning about thoughts, feelings, and behaviors in the cognitive triangle is an excellent starting point for managing your anxiety-driven anger. When you're aware of the process, you can make changes in the process. Figuring out how and when you can change your thoughts, feelings, and behaviors means that you're never stuck. It may seem like you'll always react in a certain way. You'll always have an angry response. You'll always get in trouble for your stress. You'll always tell yourself that the worst outcome is coming up. But that's not true. You get to be in charge of what you tell yourself, what you feel, and how you react. Understanding the impact all these thoughts, feelings, and behaviors have on one another also gives you so many opportunities to change. You have more power than you think.

# CHAPTER 3

# Why Anxiety and Anger Are A-OK

Anxiety, anger, and especially anxiety-driven anger can all be really uncomfortable emotions. Who likes feeling tearful, overheated, and out of control? Who wants to experience that kind of distress? Who likes having someone watch them when they are feeling scared or angry? Of course, it seems like anxiety and anger should be avoided.

The truth is these are important and healthy emotions to experience. These feelings let us know that we don't like what's going on and that we need something to change, internally or externally. When we're angry, we know there's a problem to solve, and we can either jump into that problem solving or we can take a break. When we're nervous, we know there's something that doesn't feel right; something that needs to be fixed, or something that we need to look at in a different way. Our feelings give us crucial information. So rather than trying to avoid or ignore our anger and anxiety, and the accompanying thoughts and behaviors, we need to work on gently accepting what's going on and moving forward.

Isaac Newton, that famous discoverer of gravity, talks about how every action has an equal and opposite reaction. When you push against a wall, the wall is pushing back. This is easiest to notice when you're somewhere with less friction, like on an ice rink, or wearing Rollerblades. The amount of force you're using against the wall is what propels you backward, and if that wall were on roller skates, it would be moving away from you too.

When we have a thought or emotion that feels distressing, we often try to push it away instead of listening to it. But when we try to shove away a thought, it shoves back. The harder we push against that thought or feeling, the stronger it becomes, until we feel like we're using all our mental energy to avoid difficult thoughts and emotions—just like if we're on that ice rink, skating as fast as we can into the wall, and pushing and pushing and pushing. We're just going to end up pushing ourselves to the point of falling down or even hurting ourselves.

There's a much easier way to deal with this struggle against distressing or overwhelming thoughts and feelings. We simply remove the struggle. We gently glide away on the ice. We see that it's there. We know that there's something that we might want to change, and that doesn't make our feelings bad. We don't have to fight against them.

## IGNORING THE CHOCOLATE CAKE

Struggling against thoughts and feelings really doesn't work. You may be asking, "If I don't have to fight my thoughts or feelings, even if they're bad thoughts, or even if I'm feeling really, really bad, shouldn't I just try to ignore them?" This is a super logical conclusion! Unfortunately, this isn't going to work either. Let's go through a quick exercise to see why.

Ready?

Perfect.

Here's the only direction: Don't think about chocolate cake!

…

Now ask yourself, what's the first thing that popped into your mind? If you're like most people, as soon as I told you not to think about chocolate cake, your brain started to picture it even before you could stop yourself. You may have pictured a beautifully frosted cake, or thought about how hungry you are, or remembered when your grandma would make chocolate cupcakes for your birthday. Maybe you started to picture this, and then tried to stop—but the cake is still there, getting harder and harder to ignore.

If I hadn't told you, "Don't think about this!" it likely wouldn't have been in your head at all (unless you happen to be reading this book and baking a chocolate cake at the same time). The very act of telling you not to think about something leads to the thought popping up. This means that telling your brain not to think about things doesn't really work.

Let's continue the exercise: Please continue not to think about chocolate cake. Don't think about how it smells. Don't think about how it tastes. Don't think about how much you want to eat some. Don't think about the glossy frosting, or the colorful sprinkles you would put on top. Don't think about any of it.

When you are committed to ignoring a thought or a feeling, you have to commit to ignoring every offshoot. Like if you're trying to ignore memories of an embarrassing experience, you'll probably have different parts of it come to mind, such as remembering when you wet your pants in grade school, and how it felt so uncomfortable and cold, and how the teacher looked at you, and how you didn't want to tell your parents, and how you had to take your pants home in a plastic grocery bag and borrow a too large pair of sweatpants from the school's lost and found. Whenever a new part of the embarrassing event comes to you, you're left trying to ignore that part of it, too, until you have a huge list of things you've told yourself it's not okay to think about.

Continuing with this exercise even further: Please don't think about chocolate cake. I'm begging you. If you think about chocolate cake, that means you're a bad person. It's shameful to think about chocolate cake. If you even think about thinking about chocolate cake, or the frosting, or the sprinkles, or the smell, not only are you a bad person, you're also failing at the experiment. You don't want to be a failure, do you?

Now, has my shaming you made it any easier to not think about chocolate cake? My guess is that it hasn't—if anything, it's probably made it harder and more uncomfortable. And yet, we often blame ourselves for thoughts and feelings that seem impossible to stop. Telling yourself that a thought is bad, or that you're bad for thinking it, usually makes the thought bigger. Not only are you not supposed to think about chocolate cake, you've upped the ante. You've made this more challenging by adding a value judgment on your inability to ignore the thought.

As I add more things to your "don't think about chocolate cake" list, your brain has to spend more and more time trying to avoid any related chocolate cake thoughts, and also worry about the implications of you thinking about it. What you're probably realizing as we go through this experiment is that it's actually impossible to not think about chocolate cake. You can't stop the thoughts. Especially when I keep adding prompts and reminders and details. Every single example of "don't think about it" just turns into "think about it." The more layers of prohibition you add, the more inevitable the thoughts become.

It's impossible to stop a thought from happening, right? Our brains just aren't designed this way. So instead of trying to stop or ignore thoughts, what if we tried something else instead?

## MOVING FORWARD WITH ACCEPTANCE

The only way to get through this exercise is to actually think about the chocolate cake. It's impossible not to think about it when I tell you not to! Rather than fighting or struggling against a thought, or trying to push it away, we want to use acceptance. Let's just accept that this thought is going to come up for us, instead of engaging in the struggle and trying to block every aspect of the distress.

It's like having your two fingers in a finger trap. The harder you pull your fingers apart, the tighter and tighter the trap becomes. You're fully stuck. The only way to release your fingers from the finger trap is to bring them together, loosen the trap, and gently slide each finger out. When it comes to thoughts, pulling away sharply and forcefully just tightens the trap. You're fully stuck in the thought. Instead of pulling away harder, we want to move closer. By gently coming toward the thought, noticing it, and even empathizing with it, we can release ourselves from being stuck.

What does it look like to empathize with a thought? Above, in our cake exercise, we tried doing the opposite by shaming ourselves for having the thought, telling ourselves the thought was bad, and furthermore that we were bad for having it. Shame isn't really a great tool for making our thoughts feel less distressing. Shocking, right? Shame tends to add to the suffering. Shame tells us that the thought is bad, and we're bad for having it. Shame tells us to feel guilty. So rather than shame, we want to try acceptance and kindness instead.

Picture this: You're in your room after having a fight with your parents, and you text your friend Kyla for support. Kyla doesn't text back right away, which is fine, but then you see that she's still posting on social media. Your brain may first jump to a thought like "Something is wrong." Maybe Kyla doesn't care about your problems. Maybe you upset her and she's ignoring you. Maybe this is just like that time when everyone started ignoring you in the fifth grade, and you were totally isolated and alone until you moved to a new middle school. Ugh, you hate thinking about that! You tear up and try pushing the thought away.

You don't want to have these thoughts or remember that painful time in your life. It makes you feel anxious and upset, and you're starting to spiral. You want to trust your friend because you value your friendship. So you try to distract yourself and move on to your homework, but as the hours tick by it becomes harder and harder to ignore your fears. You keep thinking about being ignored and being unliked. You end up drafting and deleting potential texts to Kyla, asking if you did something wrong, or if she's mad, or if you should even bother staying friends. Fear and frustration build, even though you hate feeling so uncomfortable. Finally, after writing and rewriting it, you text her, "Hey, you're obviously on your phone since you keep messaging people and posting stuff. I know you don't care about what's going on with me. I just want to know what I did wrong or if I shouldn't text you again."

Kyla immediately calls you and says she was trying to focus on homework, so she turned off text alerts. She says, "You always make such a big deal about nothing! We're good! You know I care about you. Let's talk." Instead of talking, though, you feel embarrassed. Why did you jump to the worst-case scenario, even when you tried not to? What's wrong with you?

What would this look like, though, if you had accepted what was going on, and had been kind to your brain as it came up with all these questions, fears, and worries? What if you had just stated the facts: "I texted my friend about a problem and she hasn't texted me back. Okay." What if you said, "Yep, here's that thought about fifth grade again. That tends to come up when I think I'm being ignored. Okay. It's not bad, it's not good, it just is." If you had noticed the thought instead of struggling with it, would it have changed the outcome? Would it have lowered the level of your emotions? Would it have changed how you reacted?

One year, my husband and I were taking down the decorations from our Christmas tree. We hadn't watered the tree in a while, so the pine needles were all super dry, and the branches had gravitated downward after that first, fresh day we put it up. We had strung lights on the tree, and then a beaded garland, and then added all the ornaments. The ornaments were easy to remove, but the beads were really stuck in the dry tree. Every time we tried to pull them out, a shower of needles fell to the floor, making a huge mess. It felt frustrating for the both of us! My husband ended up pulling the beads tighter, branches crumbling off the tree as he tugged harder and harder, and we ended up with a huge, jumbled knot. The more we got angry at the tree, and frustrated with one another, the more tangled everything became, until we both had to take a break.

I went to our bedroom and lay down on the floor, closing my eyes. I took a slow, deep breath in through my nose for four counts, holding it for four, and then breathing out through my mouth for eight counts, holding another four.

We came back to the tree after cooling down, ready to tackle the task at hand. Let me tell you, it's much easier to untangle a bunched-up knot of beaded garland when you're feeling calm. There was an extra benefit from us calming down too. We were able to do some problem solving when we no longer had that frustration clouding our minds. We realized that the lights were half out anyway, and we didn't need to save them since they were going into the trash. My husband got out the scissors, and we snipped off each section of lights so that we could easily take them off. It was so much easier to see the links between everything and disentangle the remaining decorations when we had dropped the struggle. It was still a bit of a mess, but we accepted it and were able to move forward until the job was done.

## WHAT IS ACCEPTANCE?

You're going to start noticing that this book uses the word "accept" a lot, usually in the context of accepting and moving forward. What does that mean? Why is that one of our big goals?

Acceptance means taking what is offered. Like if your grandma gave you a hand-knitted sweater for your birthday and, even though it was really itchy, you said thanks, and you even put it on to show her how much you loved it. In the psychological sense, acceptance is recognizing the reality of what's going on without trying to do anything about it. You're taking that itchy sweater, and you're not trying to make it softer, or asking your grandma to take it back, or being upset that this is the third itchy sweater in a row and you'd really love a video game or something next time. You're not mad about it. It is what it is.

Acceptance is particularly helpful when we're feeling a lot of emotional distress around our thoughts and feelings, because it helps us take a step back and just observe what's going on, without adding all this struggle on top of it. Acceptance allows the unpleasantness to exist. We can sit with those feelings or thoughts that we may not like in the moment, and sitting with them allows us to kind of detach from them. Sure, we could change them, but we don't have to. We're not trying to control ourselves. We're not trying to stop thoughts in their tracks. We're not trying to flip off the switch to our emotions. We're just feeling those feelings and thinking those thoughts, riding them like a wave as they come up and down.

A thought is just a thought. It's just our brain communicating with itself. It's a fired neuron and chemicals traveling from one synapse to another. Our brains come up with a million thoughts every single day. Acceptance would ask, what makes this distressing thought special? Probably nothing. It's just the thought that is sticking out to us in this moment. It's not bad. It's not good. It just is.

You should have as many tools available to you as you need when it comes to managing your anxiety-driven anger. Some people really like using acceptance and just noticing what's going on inside them. Other people prefer to dig in and start reframing their thoughts, changing their behaviors, and restructuring what's going on internally. There's an acceptance route and a restructuring route. Either is good! You even have the option to start down one path and then switch to the other. Different situations may call for taking different paths. Just remember that you always have a choice: to restructure your thoughts and deal with them, or to accept them and let them be.

On first glance, it may seem that cognitive restructuring is the more useful tool, because you're really digging in and purposefully coming up with different things to tell yourself. It's very action oriented. Restructuring seems like such a good, hands-on intervention. Teens with anxiety tend to like working toward something concrete. Because restructuring takes effort and practice, it can align a bit more with your anxiety's need to try to control what's going on. Acceptance seems so easy by comparison. It hardly seems like work at all. You're not really changing anything; you're just sitting with it.

Actually, acceptance can take a lot of work and effort, especially at first when you're so used to pushing thoughts away or trying to dig in further. The goal is to feel a little less entangled with our thoughts through that acceptance. So you could sit with the thought that comes up and say, "Thank you for thinking that thought. I appreciate your contribution, but I don't really need it right now." You could say the thought over and over again, like how if you say the word "banana" twenty times in a row, it ends up losing all meaning—it's just sounds. You can label the thought as a thought, rather than a fact, and just tell yourself, "I'm noticing the thought that…" You can imagine the thought just traveling past you, like a train on its tracks. There's no way you'd try to stop a train by running in front of it, right? You just let that train keep rolling.

There are two great choices here: restructuring and acceptance. Sometimes it's helpful to ask Grandma to stop giving you itchy sweaters. Sometimes it's helpful to just say thanks and move on. You get to decide what's going to be the best option for you in the moment.

## THOUGHT SPIRALS

Thoughts can start small, get bigger and bigger, and then lead to a huge, spiraling reaction. This is particularly common when it comes to anxiety. One thought leads to another and another and another, and we get caught up in an anxious, swirling spiral of thoughts that keep us from focusing on whatever else is at hand.

If you're someone who gets focused on grades and doing well in school, you might notice some anxiety about tests. You may have a thought spiral that looks something like this:

- If I get less than an A on this chemistry test, that means I have a bad grade.

- If I have a bad grade, that means I'm doing poorly in this class.

- I might even fail this class…

- And other classes…

- And I'll barely graduate high school…

- And I won't get into the college I want…

- And I won't be able to go to medical school…

- Which means I'll never be a doctor!

- My life will be ruined!

Phew, okay! Yikes! This must be the most important test of your life! Sure, it's one chemistry test, but it sounds like this test result is going to really determine your future success. It's a huge problem. These are gigantic thoughts. The potential outcome of this test could be catastrophic. Pushing the thoughts away seems impossible.

Luckily, you know you have two good options. We can go down the restructuring route, or the acceptance route. Different routes will resonate with different people, so we're going to walk through both paths.

## Restructuring Route

Let's take a step back. There's no way that getting less than an A on this test means your life is effectively ruined, right? The test may be important, and you may really want an A, but it's a huge leap to go from "If I get less than an A, that's a bad grade" to "I won't get into medical school or be a doctor, and my life will be ruined!"

On the restructuring route, the first step when you notice you're spiraling is to explore the thoughts and ask some follow-up questions. You can start at any point of your thought spiral. Ask yourself:

- Is this thought true?

- Even if it is, is it, like, 100 percent true or more like 50 percent true?

- What else could be true?

- Is this thought helpful right now?

- Is there something more helpful I could tell myself in this moment?

You're always welcome to come up with a few options of other, more helpful thoughts, until you find something that really clicks with you.

Let's go through this with our anxiety thought spiral above. "If I get less than an A on this test, that means I have a bad grade, and in conclusion, I won't be a doctor and my life will be ruined." Is this thought true? Less than an A isn't necessarily a bad grade, even if it's not ideal. Even if you failed, one failing grade doesn't mean you won't get to go to medical school. Not being a doctor isn't the end of the world.

Is it 100 percent true that anything less than an A is a bad grade? Maybe it's not your favorite grade, but it's not the absolute worst to get less than an A.

What else could be true? Well, even if you get less than an A, you will probably still get into a pretty good school.

Is it helpful to tell yourself that getting less than an A on this test is going to ruin your life? Not really. This kind of thought is upping the stakes of the test so much that you're probably not going to focus on answering the questions.

What's something more helpful you could tell yourself in this moment? You could say, "Yes, I'm worried about this test, and I also know that I'm just going to do the best that I can." You could also say, "I want to be a doctor, so I know my tests are important, but they're not the end of the world. I'll have tons of opportunities to prove myself before it's time to even think about applying to med school."

We know from our cake example that just ignoring this thought spiral wouldn't do much. We also know that shaming ourselves for having thoughts like this would just make it harder to get through the test without freaking out. So we restructure the thoughts until we end up at a place where we can feel better about what we're saying to ourselves, and we can refocus on the task at hand.

## Acceptance Route

Going down the acceptance route means you recognize that you have very limited control over what thoughts come up for you. Things pop up in your brain all the time. This is totally okay. It's normal.

With this particular thought spiral, you start by recognizing that your brain is trying to protect you by preparing for the worst-case scenario. You don't need to pass judgment on your brain for coming up with these thoughts. You know that being upset with your brain just makes it harder to move past the problem.

Next, even though you know your brain is just trying to do its job, you also want to let this thought spiral take a back seat and get out of the way. You have the option to intervene here to explore the thought using the restructuring questions, and you also have the option to disengage. Instead of asking yourself how true or helpful the thoughts are, you do something totally different. You tell yourself, "I'm noticing that I'm having a lot of thoughts about this test, and it's kind of leading to an anxious thought spiral. Okay. It makes sense to be nervous about the test."

You sit with the thoughts a little longer. "I'm going to take a pause and notice these thoughts… Yes, here's a thought about my test. Here's a thought I'm telling myself about college. Hmm, here's another thought about my future."

Next, you could use your repetition tool (remember the banana exercise a few pages ago?), where you say the thought over and over again until it loses all meaning. You repeat to yourself, "If I get a B, I'm going to fail. If I get a B, I'm going to fail. If I get a B, I'm going to fail," until the words are just sounds your mouth is making. Saying it a ton of times doesn't make it truer. This whole time, the thought was just something your synapses were firing off.

Next, you let these thoughts pass by. "All right, one at a time, I can let each of these thoughts go. If they come up again, I can let them go again, as many times as I need to." Rather than picking up each thought, questioning it, and exploring it, you just disconnect.

You might also like incorporating a visualization into this process. Because you are acknowledging thoughts and letting them gently go, you could picture each thought being encircled by a red balloon. Imagine letting that balloon go and watching it gently float away. When another thought comes up, let that thought be encircled by another balloon, maybe an orange one this time. You let that orange balloon gently float away too. Let's say another thought comes up—imagine this thought going into a nice, yellow balloon. Let that yellow balloon go, and watch it gently float away. Keep repeating with different balloons and different colors as many times as needed. As each thought floats away, notice a sense of calm coming over more and more of your body.

## The Hybrid Route

You always have a choice to restructure your thoughts or to accept them. You can also do both! That's where our hybrid route comes in. It's the *"and"* option. Both things can be true.

You notice that you're having a thought spiral. You start with a restructuring tool and decide if this thought spiral is helpful or unhelpful. You follow up with some gentle redirection while still having a lot of compassion for your brain. You might add in something like, "It's okay to have these thoughts, and at the same time, these thoughts aren't super helpful when it comes to concentrating on the test." Then, you decide what to do: spend more time on the thoughts or just gently let them go.

You might tell yourself, "Getting less than an A on this test probably isn't a bad grade, *and* I know that worrying about my grade before taking the test doesn't really help. So, let's focus on just taking the test first."

You could say, "Yes, this test might impact my future and my goal of being a doctor, *and* at the same time, it's just one test of many."

You can also focus on the feelings that come up with this thought spiral, telling yourself, "I'm feeling really anxious about the test, which might make it harder to focus, *and* I know that anxiety is okay. I'm just going to surf this wave and be with it. I know that my anxiety might get bigger, but it will also go back down."

# THE CHOICE IS YOURS

We know there's a big difference between pushing thoughts away and gently letting them go. You want to cultivate this sense of ease that comes with not fighting against your thoughts. None of your restructuring, acceptance, or hybrid routes involve shaming your brain, ignoring what's going on, or trying to cover up what your brain is saying.

As you continue to go through this book, you'll notice that it mostly uses the hybrid route. I really like the "*and*" option; it allows for a lot of flexibility in dealing with anxious, angry, overwhelming thoughts and thought spirals. You don't like feeling anxious, *and* you know it's okay to feel this way. Your brain is coming up with an unhelpful thought, *and* you know that you don't have to change that thought, you can just let it be.

Our biggest goal is to not add extra, unnecessary suffering to the problems we face. Just know that these routes—restructuring, acceptance, and hybrid—open up a whole ton of pathways for you when it comes to managing what's going on for you.

## CHAPTER 4

# Figure Out Your Explosion Point

Everyone has a limit. We deal with the anxiety, frustration, and stress that comes up every day of our lives, and eventually, we just can't handle it anymore. Our calm, collected bodies and brains give way to big outbursts, yelling, scream‑ing, maybe even cursing at our friends or parents.

While it may feel at times like your angry/anxious outburst comes out of nowhere, that's not actually true. Your emotions are bubbling up underneath the surface, even outside of your conscious awareness.

Think about a glass of water. We add a little stress, and the glass gets a little fuller. We experience a big stress, and maybe we fill up that glass all the way to the top. All it takes is a few more drops for that glass to overflow. Your emotional tolerance works exactly like this glass of water. As stressful things happen, your water level gets higher and higher. Once you reach that very top of your emotional tolerance glass, it would take just one more drop of stress for that water to spill over. This is where you'll notice your emotional outbursts happening. Those emotions that you were able to keep internal are now pouring out everywhere—and making a big mess.

What helps? You might think a big mess needs a big fix, but it's a lot easier than that. We lower the water level by doing things that help calm us down. Going on a walk might help you drain a few milliliters. Talking to a friend who really gets you could take out a big glug. The most important part is to be aware of the water level, and to recognize what triggers your stress to fill up and what helps your stress to go back down. If you know you're getting close to that over-flow point, you can make sure you're proactively dealing with what's going on.

## BIG, MEDIUM, AND SMALL

We all have different levels of emotions. For now, let's categorize these into big, medium, and small. You need to figure out what these levels mean to you, because everyone has a different personal limit. You want to clue in to when an emotion feels small and manageable, medium and a little more challenging, or too big to handle. Imagine your glass just having a bit of water, compared to more at the middle level, and then compared to being filled right to the top of your glass. Your glass may be bigger or smaller than other people's glasses, and that's okay. We're all individuals.

Think about an event where you felt angry. Bring that mad feeling into your body. Add details to the event as you think about it. Who was there? What happened? Where were you? When did this occur? Why did it make you angry? Get really specific as you remember this thing that happened. Sit with this anger for a minute. Now taking a step back, how mad were you in the moment? Were you just a little mad? Were you out-of-control, explosively angry? Or were you somewhere in the middle? Why?

What about the last time you felt anxious? What happened? What seemed to trigger that anxious feeling? How anxious did you feel? Was it just a small twinge of anxious feeling? Was it so big that you felt totally overwhelmed? Or was it somewhere in between?

Imagine this: You feel like you're often being compared to your older brother, Matt, by your parents and teachers, and even by yourself. One day in class, your teacher hands you back a graded paper and says, "This was pretty good for you! Matt was such a pleasure to have in my class last year, so I hope that I can see even better work from you moving forward." This comment echoes around your head for the rest of the school day, getting louder and louder. As soon as you get home, you head to your brother's room and pound on his door. When he opens it, you can't help but yell, "You think you're so great, but you're not!" He just smirks and asks, "Another tough day at school, bud?" You truly hate him.

Let's look at your emotions. You might feel angry, and you might also feel some anxiety in that comparison to Matt. Is your anger in this moment big, medium, or small? This is a personal question. For you, yelling might only happen when you're experiencing a big amount of anger. Others might yell even at that medium anger level. What about any anxiety you feel about being as good as Matt, or as smart as Matt, or having your teachers like you as much as they seem to like Matt? Does that anxiety seem pretty small? Or is it the kind of anxiety that you notice becoming bigger and bigger, as you hear more and more about how great your brother was?

As you become more aware of your personal experience with emotions and your own emotional limits, you can start to expand your scale from big, medium, and small to allow for a more nuanced take on what's going on for you. Building your awareness is the goal, because knowing what is going on for you emotionally makes it easier to recognize your triggers and responses, and even curb what's happening.

## IS YOUR CUP OVERFLOWING?

As you think about your big, medium, and small emotions, you can also explore your level of emotional tolerance. Picture yourself going to an ice cream shop. If you order a large chocolate shake, and they only have small cups, your large, sticky shake is going to spill all over the counter. That cup just doesn't have the capacity to handle it. If you were to order a small shake, and they only had large cups available, it's a nonissue. That drink fits easily.

Recognizing when you're about to be emotionally overwhelmed is a good first step to keeping the messes from happening. It's like interrupting that server behind the counter and saying, "Whoa! That shake's not going to fit in that cup! Can we pause for a second?" You deal with the emotions that are happening before they overflow and spill out.

Another option is to start building your level of emotional tolerance and make your cup size larger. You can handle more emotional stressors by regularly practicing relaxation strategies, which you'll learn about in the next chapter.

You may notice that there are people in your life who seem unfazed by everything. They seem to get through any challenge they face. This doesn't mean that they're not impacted by the world around them, or that they don't also deal with being sad, hurt, anxious, or angry. Stressors still accumulate for them, because it's impossible to not be impacted by the world around you. They just have a larger cup. They can hold more of that chocolate shake than you can.

If you're a small-cup person and you'd like to be a large-cup person, you can work on it. You're not stuck as a small-cup forever. You need to understand what overflows your cup and how to stop the overflow from happening, and to build up your coping skills. All three of these areas will help the size of your cup increase—maybe just a little at a time, but enough to make a difference.

## THE WINDOW OF TOLERANCE

Your small emotions can grow, and your big emotions can shrink. There's an easy way to visually track this increase and decrease in our emotional levels that's called "the window of tolerance" (Ogden, Minton, and Pain 2006; Siegel 2012). The window of tolerance represents our stress state and is a great way to show the number of things we can tolerate before we get totally overwhelmed.

There are two zones to the window of tolerance—the high, hyperarousal zone and the low, hypoarousal zone. In the hyper zone, we find our overwhelming anxiety-based emotions, which increase our heart rate and breathing (like the fight-flight-or-freeze response). Hyperarousal, moving up that window, happens when we're feeling anxious or angry or overwhelmed. The other zone is hypoarousal, which encapsulates those emotions that really lower our heart rate, breathing rate, and energy. This is when we feel like we're shutting down and need to totally disengage, and usually correlates with feelings of sadness or even depression. As events happen over the course of our day, we track up or track down. Generally, we stay within the window. As soon as we cross over our top or bottom barrier, we're in full-blown freak-out or shut-down mode. It's a lot more comfortable to operate in the middle of our window. If we're staying within the top or bottom barriers, we're able to tolerate what's going on.

Let's walk you through an example of the window of tolerance, so you can see how to use this tool to represent what's happening, emotionally, for you.

You wake up and realize you slept through your 6:30 a.m. alarm. Automatically, yikes! You feel a big spike in anxiety and jump up on your window of tolerance. Luckily, you soon realize that it's a late-start day: 9:00 a.m. instead of the usual 7:30. Even though it's already 8:00 a.m., it's not a big deal. You travel back down into that comfortable middle range of your window. Sure, you notice a little anxiety about feeling more rushed, but you know you're not in trouble, and you're looking forward to the shorter day of school.

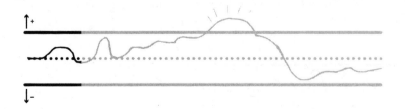

Things don't always stay resolved, even if you feel calmer on your own. Let's say, after you get ready, you come downstairs for breakfast. Your mom yells at you for sleeping past your alarm again and says you have to get yourself to school because she's leaving for work right now. You had calmed down about sleeping in, but now there's another anxiety spike, and you feel frustrated with your mom and with yourself. You snap back at her that she should have just woken you up if it was such a big deal, and surprisingly, she apologizes and agrees. You calm back down again.

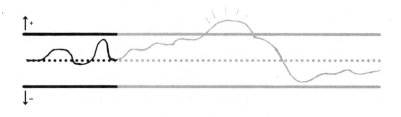

Sometimes, stressors can start to pile up, as you'll see below. On your way to school, still kind of annoyed about this morning and your fight with your mom, you realize that you actually forgot to complete a piece of homework for your first class of the day, biology, which bumps up your stress level, as you'll see on the window of tolerance below, labeled "a." When you get to your biology classroom early, intending to finish the homework, your teacher announces there's a pop quiz (b). Oh, and you have to turn in the homework you forgot right now (c). That medium anxiety has turned into big anxiety.

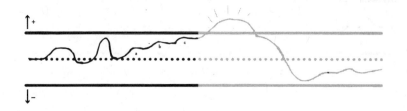

As you can see, you're right at the top of your window of tolerance, primed for an anxious/angry/out-of-control outburst. So when your teacher comes up to you and says, "You forgot to do the homework? That's not like you!" it's a small additional stress, but it tips the scales enough that you're at your explosion point, outside your window of tolerance

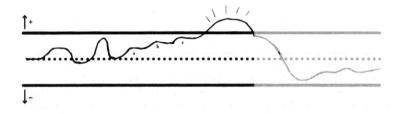

You shout at your teacher, "I never forgot it before! I can't believe you expected us to do homework and be ready for a pop quiz! That's so unfair!" You notice that you're starting to have trouble catching your breath. Maybe you even notice a combination of that anxious internal feeling and that angry external expression, experiencing a panicky feeling about your mistake while huffing and puffing about how stupid this class is. Because you've breached the top edge of your window of tolerance, you're on that hyperarousal side, and you're feeling all those explosive fight-flight-or-freeze reactions happening in your brain and body.

After your explosion, though, you take a step back and your body naturally sinks you back within your window. You never stay out of your window of tolerance forever. Your teacher gives you *a look* and says, "Let's talk about this after class." Your classmates and even your crush seem to be staring at you (d). It feels impossible to refocus and take the pop quiz. You're too embarrassed about the yelling. Actually, you just feel pretty terrible about the whole event overall. You don't know what's wrong with you. You just keep repeating to yourself: "I'm awful. I'm awful. I'm awful." As you continue to engage in this critical self-talk, you lose more and more steam, dropping lower and lower down in your window (e), and that depressive turn makes it hard for you to even finish up the quiz. You feel too awful to focus, so you put down your pencil and stare at the floor until it's time to leave. By the time you go up to your teacher's desk at the end of class, you can't even look at her when she asks, "Hey, what's going on with you today?"

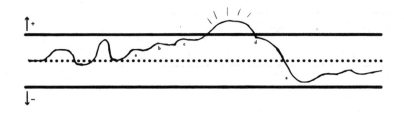

## THE TAKEAWAYS

As you look through this example, I want you to notice a few things:

- Just like in life, there are multiple stressful things happening, all within the course of one morning. It's not just that one thing happens, and the rest of your day you're totally mellow and traveling smack-dab through the middle of your window of tolerance. Things happen all the time, and even if they're small stressors, or you notice a little anxiety or a little anger, that feeling can build when the next challenge comes your way. The effect of stress is cumulative.

- Those bumps up your window depend entirely on what's stress-triggering for you. Some people won't get as stressed out about missing their alarm or could care less about forgetting a homework assignment. You probably know someone who always seems cool, calm, and collected.

That doesn't mean that they don't have their own window of tolerance and nothing stresses them out. It just means that either those things don't move them up too high on their window, or it could also mean that their window of tolerance is just a lot bigger than yours.

- There were several points during the morning that you could have intervened and redirected your trajectory to stay within your window of tolerance. You couldn't change the situation and what happened, but as you know, you are the one in charge of your thoughts, feelings, and reactions. This part is crucial! You can use this empowerment to review the trajectory and figure out at which points in time it may be helpful to take a step back, cool down, or do something different in order to redirect where you're going, and maybe even stop yourself from reaching your explosion point.

Now it's your turn. Grab a piece of paper and draw two straight, horizontal lines running across it, and a dotted line along the middle, just like this:

Bring to mind a recent event that stressed you out so much that you reached your explosion point. As always, we want to bring a lot of details into the memory, so sit a moment to think about the who, what, where, when, and why of the event. What happened before? What happened after?

After you have a clear memory of this event, let's start tracking before, during, and after the event on your window of tolerance, just as we did in the previous example. When you started that day, where were you on your window of tolerance? Tracking along that morning, what happened next? Did you notice your emotions spike up on that hyperarousal zone, or slide down toward that hypoarousal zone? After that first spike, did you return to the middle of your window, or did something else happen? Did you reach your explosion point quickly, or did several things happen first? How far along your window of tolerance did it take for you to calm back down after exploding? Where were you on your window afterward?

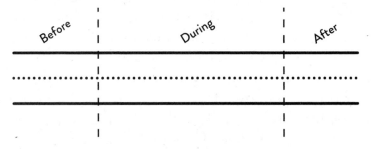

When you've finished drawing out your window, let's see what you notice. I could ask a thousand different questions here, but the most important one is: What does this window tell you about yourself?

Does it show you something important about how you respond to stressors? Does it say something to you about what you could change? Having the data in front of us gives us a chance to interpret it. When we can clearly see what is happening and how it impacts us emotionally, we can be more intentional about how we respond to things moving forward. This information allows us to be more reflective, instead of just feeling like our explosive outbursts are happening out of nowhere.

## COPING SKILLS AND YOUR WINDOW OF TOLERANCE

You may notice that you reach your explosion point a lot. Things happen and build, and then you feel explosively anxious and angry. There's a way to curb these explosions before they happen, though, and even a way to build your window of tolerance so that you can handle more stressors without feeling totally overwhelmed.

Looking at the window you created above, when could you have done something to calm down, like taking some deep breaths, letting your muscles soften, or coming up with a soothing image in your mind? Take a pencil and place an X where you think these relaxation points could have been.

When I do this exercise in therapy sessions, teens often place their Xs at the top of their explosion points. This makes sense! You're overwhelmed, so it must be time to calm down, right? Actually, it's a lot more effective to proactively incorporate a coping skill. So, rather than waiting until you're right at the top of your emotional wave, you want to intervene a little earlier.

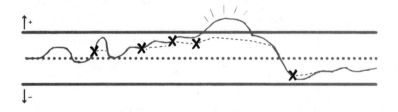

You'll notice that using that coping skill when you're rising up your emotional level catches you before you reach an explosion point. The rises and falls of the dotted line show that you will still feel angry, anxious, or overwhelmed, but the coping skill helps soften that emotional intensity and can even prevent you from getting outside your window of tolerance. Because you used pencil above, I want you to erase and replace your original Xs, if needed, and add in the dotted line to show how your emotional level may have changed following that incorporation of coping skills.

When we're looking at our new drawings, it seems so easy, right? Just add in a few coping skills and we'll never feel overwhelmed again! We're set!

Unfortunately, life is not that easy, and this takes practice and time. Don't beat yourself up if this is challenging. Why might it be hard to just do this?

- We don't always know when we're getting high up on our window of tolerance. Remember how we talk about big, medium, and small emotions? We have to catch ourselves reaching our different levels, and build in our own internal sensor.

- Even if we know we're at a medium or big emotional level, it's much harder to calm down when we're already stressed out. Just one coping skill might not cut it. We may need to stack a few of those Xs on top of one another to really change the curve.

- Our brains and our bodies are used to exploding. You've had years of experience of riding that wave up over the top of your window. We're learning an entirely new skill set, so your brain and body may still carry you over the top of your window even when you're trying to calm down. This is okay.

- Our critical self-talk can hold us back from making progress. If we continue to notice ourselves exploding, even when we're trying to use more coping skills, we can feel hopeless. You may even ask yourself, "What's the point?" Ride past this concern. Remember that real change takes a while to happen and to stick.

- Finally, you might feel self-conscious about using a coping skill in front of others. Your anxiety could be telling you that everyone is watching your deep breaths, or people think you're weird because you're closing your eyes to try to focus on slowing down your heartbeat and relaxing your muscles. When you're higher up into that big level of anxiety, that self-consciousness may be big. Do your best to focus on your internal physical experience rather than worrying about others judging you. Try and turn down that outside noise.

The more you use your coping skills, the less often you'll reach your explosion point on your window of tolerance. You'll curb your emotions sooner before they reach the top of your window. You'll notice that stressors affect you less. You'll start to feel like you're expanding your window of tolerance when you're regularly practicing ways to calm down. You can handle more and more events without feeling as ready to blow up.

In the second half of this book, we're going to work together to build up your emotional tolerance through coping skills (Chapter 5) and problem solving (Chapter 6), bringing everything together in Chapter 7, and helping you get clarity on your path forward in Chapter 8. Real change can happen. You can't change what happens to you, but you can change how you respond to it. You can be aware of your explosion point. You can even grow so that your explosion point gets further and further away.

Check in with yourself right now. Are you worried? Are you stressed? Are you thinking about your anxiety-driven anger? Or are you feeling hopeful? Put one hand on your heart and one hand on your stomach. Take a big breath in through your nose and breathe it out through your mouth. Feel how steady your heartbeat is. Recognize how strong you are. You can do this.

CHAPTER 5

# Take a Deep Breath—It's Time for Coping Skills!

Before we solve a problem, we need to understand it. That's why we've spent the previous chapters exploring the mechanisms of anxiety-driven anger, exploring our internal experience of emotions, and tracking our emotional responses through our window of tolerance. We understand the problem: Basically, our anxiety that's already there is impacted by outside stressors. These stressors bump up the severity level of our anxiety, making us more likely to explode for seemingly small things. With anxiety and stress as an undercurrent, our outbursts can look like "classic" anxiety, or they can look like anxiety-driven anger.

We understand what's going on. We're ready to change (right?). So let's talk about how coping skills can help us curb our angry/anxious responses rather than feeling like those responses are taking over. We want to learn strategies to cope with our overwhelming angry/anxious outbursts.

## EMOTIONS ELEVATORS!

(Dear reader, this is the only subhead in the whole book that involves an exclamation point, because I love emotions elevators *so much*, and I'm so excited for you to learn about them!)

Elevators, as you know, go in two directions. They go up and they come back down, and they can stop at any floor in between.

Emotions work the same way. Our emotions start at the bottom of our elevator, a low level when we're just starting to notice how we feel. As our emotions feel bigger and bigger, we're traveling up that elevator. We may stop at an emotional level before we reach the top, but as our elevator goes higher and higher and our emotions get more intense, we eventually reach the very top and we explode. We've reached our "all the way overwhelmed" point.

If you've ever experienced a panic attack before, you know how severe that anxiety can feel. You become so anxious that you feel like you can't breathe, your brain feels blank, and you think you might even die. It's terrifying. Of course, a panic attack won't kill you. It just might feel that way. That panic attack is occurring at the very top of your anxiety elevator—a 10 out of 10. Even when your anxiety feels this severe (and if you've had a panic attack, you know how severe they seem), you're not going to stay at a 10 out of 10 forever; your body can't sustain it. Over time, your body will regulate you enough to bring down your panic to a more tolerable level. It may take a while to lower on its own, but it happens.

Many people don't really notice how they're feeling until they are at the midpoint or higher on their emotions elevator. If your anxiety-driven anger seems like it makes you explode all the time, you're probably one of these people. You're not noticing your anxiety, anger, or stress until you're at a point on the elevator where it's much harder to calm down and turn it around.

Another option could be that your elevator runs fast, meaning you might notice your emotions elevator when it's on a lower level, but it gets so high so quickly that you feel like you can't catch yourself and calm down before you reach your explosion point. Every now and then, you may explode with an angry outburst, seemingly out of nowhere. You probably won't be surprised to learn that I think this is an anxiety issue rather than an anger issue. Your body and brain are so used to quickly responding to anxiety and stress that it comes out as anger. But by training you to identify these emotional levels, even if you feel like you're flying through them too fast to stop yourself, we're helping to retrain your brain.

## Your Anger Elevator

First we're going to look at your anger elevator, identifying different emotional levels.

Find another spare piece of paper, and start by drawing a narrow, tall rectangle. On this rectangle, put 1 all the way at the bottom, 5 near the middle, and 10 on top, and then fill in the rest of the numbers.

When you're at a 1 out of 10 on your anger elevator, you have just noticed a very low level of anger. Write down what you notice when you first recognize that you're feeling angry. How do you feel on the inside when you're just a bit angry? How do you look on the outside? What behaviors do you start to show, if any?

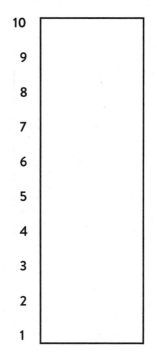

Next, let's look at that 10 out of 10 anger, all the way at the top. This is when you're so angry that you've exploded. Your anger is absolutely out of control. How does that explosive anger feel on the inside? How does it look on the outside? Write that one down at the 10 level.

Now we're going to figure out how you can tell you're at a 5 on your anger elevator. How can you tell that your anger is a little elevated, but still in that manageable, 5 out of 10 range? Write down those details next to the 5.

Continue to add to these levels, exploring how your elevator feels between that 1–5 and 5–10 range. Be sure to also identify your individual tipping point—the point on your elevator where it feels like you won't be able to turn your anger response around.

## Your Stress Elevator

Using your anger elevator as a reference, I want you to create your stress elevator. It may look something like this:

# Stress

| | |
|---|---|
| 10 | Screaming |
| 9 | Sobbing |
| 8 | Breathing stops |
| 7 | Start to cry |
| 6 | Feeling sick |
| 5 | Toes curl |
| 4 | Breathing fast |
| 3 | Tense jaw |
| 2 | Heart rate |
| 1 | Fists |

Remember, your emotional experience is your own. You should be editing this elevator to represent your personal experience with stress, including different body clues as needed, or marking down your personal tipping point. For some, stress and anxiety feel like the same emotion; and for others, including those who experience more anxiety-driven anger, there's a big difference between stress and anxiety. Typically, stress is the variable you can track most easily when you're working on building up your relaxation skills, but coping with emotions is helpful with, well, every emotion. Coping skills are there to lower the emotional intensity of anger, sadness, frustration, anxiety, and everything else.

With your stress elevator in front of you, ask yourself: In this very moment, where am I on my stress elevator? Mark down this level on a piece of paper. If you're between two numbers on your elevator, note that too. After each relaxation activity we practice, we're going to track any impact on our stress level, in either direction. Does it get better and lower where you're at on your elevator? Does it feel worse, and you've traveled up your elevator? This information is crucial to tailoring your coping skills plan for you.

## SETTING YOURSELF UP FOR SUCCESS

It's crucial to practice these coping skills before you need them, so you know what to do in the moment. Knowing how and when to use the skills make them much easier to apply. However, you'll also see a significant benefit and increase in your sense of relaxation if you start incorporating these coping skills into your life on an ongoing basis, even at times when you're not feeling particularly heightened levels of anxiety, stress, or anger.

It's like dealing with a dam. On some days, that dam holds just a small trickle of water, and other days, the water is so high that it might almost flood into the surrounding area. The dam holds the water back, but it's also designed to release water at a slower, more manageable pace, so as not to overwhelm the waterway system.

Regular practice of relaxation is just like slowly releasing the water from the dam. Using these skills proactively means you're releasing the water when it's at lower, more manageable levels, rather than waiting for the huge storm that might overflow the dam. You've taken care of the smaller amount of water so that you can handle a big influx.

We don't always know when our next stressor will happen, just like we don't always know when the next big rainstorm is going to roll in. We can make a pretty good prediction about the weather, and about the types of things that will stress us out, but sometimes things just come out of nowhere. When you're proactively using these coping skills, you're setting yourself up for success in advance of the next huge downpour. You've released enough of your stress to make room for more.

As you complete these activities and identify your favorites, think about the best way to incorporate these into your everyday life. Yes, it's great to use these coping skills to relax in the moment when you need to cool down and lower your elevator. It's also great to use these skills and lower your emotions elevator before you really need to. The easiest way to do this is to set specific times in your schedule for practice.

Some of the teens I've worked with have loved setting up a nightly meditation for themselves, once they're in bed with the lights off. Others start every cheer meet with ten deep breaths, and some begin each school day with a progressive muscle relaxation. It's easy to incorporate small things throughout your day. When you do, you can make a big difference.

## BREATHING, MUSCLES, AND MINDFULNESS

I'm going to break down coping skills into three different sections: breathing activities, muscle activities, and mindfulness and meditation activities. You'll get a chance to practice skills from all three to find what works best for you.

You may find it helpful to review your Chapter 2 body clues drawing (or journaling) activity to refresh yourself on what specific parts of your body you want to check in with, and learn what cluster of relaxation activities is likely to best work for you. The three clusters are:

- Breathing activities focus more on breathwork (shocking, I know). These activities should be especially helpful if you noticed a lot of emotional clues around your breathing—whether that breathing felt really fast or so slow that you worried it would stop—when you did the body clues activity in Chapter 2.

- Muscle activities focus on decreasing muscle tension. These tools are especially helpful if you hold a lot of stress, anger, or anxiety in your body, or if you notice an urge to hit, kick, or punch things when you're overwhelmed.

- Meditation and mindfulness activities are great to use if your anxiety and anger lead to anxiety spirals and a rush of overwhelming thoughts, or if your mind feels hyperfocused on what's making you upset.

Different coping skills work differently for different people. We're all beautiful, special individuals! It stands to reason that we need to design a relaxation plan that works for our personal needs. While one section may be a better fit for you than the others, I want you to practice all the skills described in this chapter. We need to figure out what feels most effective for you, when, and why. You're not likely to use these skills when you need them if you don't connect to them.

In addition to finding out what's most effective for you, it's also super important to regularly practice these skills. It's so much easier to recall a coping skill when you need it if you've already got it prepped and ready to go in your back pocket, rather than trying to read these instructions while you're in the middle of a freak-out-style, explosive anxiety attack.

# BREATHING ACTIVITIES

When your body experiences stress and anxiety, your breathing rate typically increases. For some with severe anxiety or a history of panic attacks, it may even feel like your breathing stops entirely. Moving to purposeful breathing helps your body slow down and center itself. It's also really useful for helping your brain focus on something other than what's making you feel stressed, anxious, or angry.

> ✱ *Remember to track the effectiveness of these skills using your stress elevator! Right now, where's your stress level at on a 1–10 scale?* ✱

## Diaphragmatic Breathing

When you're out for a run, you're breathing fast because your body is hard at work. Typically, our breathing matches this elevated rate when we experience stress. When we're calm and relaxed, like when we're sleeping, our breathing is much slower and lower.

Diaphragmatic breathing brings your breath down low into your belly, where your diaphragm muscle supports your lungs. Practice taking a slow breath in through your nose, and release it through your mouth. Then another nice, slow breath in through your nose, and then gently sigh it out through your mouth, and repeat three more times. Notice the cool air that travels in through your nose and the warm air that comes out through your mouth.

You should feel the breath traveling all the way down into your belly as you continue to slowly breathe in through your nose and out through your mouth. It can be helpful to place your hands gently on your stomach so that you feel it expand with each in-breath, letting you know that your diaphragmatic breaths are full enough to be effective.

*Remember we want to track the effectiveness of these skills using your stress elevator. Did your stress elevator go higher, lower, or stay the same after this activity?* *

## Heart and Belly Breathing

Diaphragmatic breathing is our foundational breathing skill. Heart and belly breathing takes this a step further by adding *grounding*. Grounding just means that we connect with our physical bodies in the moment, rather than getting caught up in our brain's stressed-out, worried, and overwhelmed what-ifs.

Place one hand on your heart and one hand on your belly. Take a slow breath in through your nose and release it through your mouth. Just like in diaphragmatic breathing, you should feel your belly gently rising with each breath in, and gently relaxing with each breath out. If you feel your belly going in with your in-breath and out with your out-breath, pause and try again. If it feels challenging, try lying on your back with a pillow on your belly. Focus on moving that pillow up on the in-breath and down on the out-breath.

As you become comfortable with this technique, close your eyes and focus on how that breath feels traveling through your lungs. Imagine it gently circling around from your throat to your heart and your belly, and gently traveling back up and out through your body, releasing any tension or stress it comes across. As it travels in, envision it bringing in fresh, clean air, then carrying out the good, used air as it travels out.

## Eight-Count Breaths

Some brains relax better when we give them something specific to focus on. With eight-count breaths, we build on our breathing skills above and add in counting. You'll slowly breathe in through your nose for three counts, pause for one, and then let the breath travel out through your mouth for four counts.

Here's how I count it out: Breathe in through your nose, two, three; pause; and then breathe out through your mouth for five, six, seven, eight. In, two, three; pause; and out five, six, seven, eight.

Make sure that you're not speeding up and counting too fast, like, "one-twothreefourfivesixseveneight," and that you're not counting so slowly that your breath feels like it's being restricted. Just focus on breathing, gentle and steady. It may be helpful to set a metronome to a slow pace.

Repeat until you notice yourself lowering on your stress elevator.

A note about eight-count breaths: Some brains can get really fixated on numbers and rule following, especially when they are anxious brains. If your mind starts to feel like you *have to* breathe for eight counts, or if you have trouble returning to your normal breathing after this activity, just focus on making sure you breathe in slowly, pause, and breathe out slowly for just a bit longer, without counting out the numbers. This approach is equally effective.

✳ Effectiveness check-in: *Which breathing activity lowered your stress elevator the most? Which one do you want to continue to use going forward?* ✳

## MUSCLE ACTIVITIES

Muscle-focused relaxation activities help you notice and loosen tension in your muscles. If you tend to hold yourself rigid as your stress level increases, you'll be able to help unclench your muscles. A lot of times, we don't even notice our muscle tension as it slowly adds up over time.

In this moment, notice your posture. Notice how close your shoulders are to your ears. So many people hold stress in this area, and those shoulders creep higher and higher up over the course of a stressful day. Just noticing this helps you to soften them.

✱ *Remember to track the effectiveness of these skills using your stress elevator! Right now, where's your stress level at on a 1–10 scale?* ✱

## Body Scan

Where do you hold tension in your body? Let's move through your different muscle groups to explore this, and make sure we're targeting specific areas. For the first few times, read through this activity as you use it; in the future, you can do this scan with your eyes closed, making it easier to focus on what's going on internally.

Sitting on a chair, or lying on your bed, make sure your arms and your legs are uncrossed.

Starting at the top of your head, notice any tension you might be holding in your face, your forehead, or your jaw. If you notice any small tension, even just holding your jaw a little clenched, or sticking your tongue to the roof of your mouth, let that tension soften and relax.

Move down to your neck and your shoulders, letting any tension drop. Move down your arms, forearms, and hands, noting and releasing any tension.

From the base of your throat, move your attention to your chest and torso, your heartbeat, your breathing, letting everything feel steady and soft. Move down to your abdomen, relaxing any tightness you notice in the muscles around your belly.

Then, travel your attention down all the vertebrae along your back until you reach the base of your spine, noticing and releasing any tightness. Bring your attention down to your hips, where a lot of us hold on to stress, and then down the back of your legs and the front of your legs, smoothing and softening out all those muscles with your mind.

Finally, notice your feet, from your heels to your arches and all the way to your toes. Let any remaining tension in any of your muscles release.

**✻** *Following this body scan, where's your stress level at on a 1–10 scale?* **✻**

## Progressive Muscle Relaxation

Muscles tense up when our fight-flight-or-freeze response is activated; purposely helping those muscles relax and soften lets our brain know that we can be safe and calm rather than feeling on edge.

This activity is easiest to practice the first time when you're lying down on your bed or on a couch, but you're also welcome to do it while sitting. Just make sure to uncross your legs and arms, and keep both feet on the ground to start.

First, curl your toes and hold them for five counts. Let them release.

Next, point your toes to flex your calves, and hold for five, four, three, two, one, and then let those relax.

Squeeze the backs of your thighs and hold them together for five, four, three, two, one, and then let them release, feeling your legs soften back into your bed, couch, or chair.

Crunch the muscles in your abdomen and hold for five, four, three, two, one, and then let your abdominal muscles soften and relax.

Tense your shoulders up to your ears for five, four, three, two, one, and then let your shoulders gently drop back down.

Tighten your arms, while keeping your hands loose, almost like you're lifting weights. Hold your arms tight for five, four, three, two, one, and then soften.

Squeeze your hands tightly for five, four, three, two, one, and then let them loosen.

Next, scrunch up all the muscles in your face, almost like you just ate a super sour lemon. Hold them taut for five, four, three, two, one, and then let them relax.

Finally, squeeze all your muscles, all at once. Tighten everything up for five, four, three, two, one, and then—ahhh!—let all your muscles relax and soften. Shake out your shoulders and your arms, and let your body wiggle a little. Feel yourself fully sinking into your spot. If any muscles feel a little sore or tight, gently massage them or stretch a bit.

## Squeezing Lemons

It's wonderful when you can cycle through the whole progressive muscle relaxation script. In class, though, scrunching up your entire face can feel a little silly. That's where squeezing lemons come in. Rather than going through all your muscles, you're just going to focus on squeezing your fists tightly, like you're squeezing lemons for lemonade, holding them for five counts, and then releasing them and shaking them out. Repeat this sequence two more times.

The great thing about squeezing lemons is that it's easy to do under the radar. Remember that people often interpret certain actions as angry, so showing everyone your tightly squeezed fists may make them a little leery of what you're going to do next. Instead, you can discreetly tighten your fists and let them loose in an out-of-sight area—for example, down by your sides or under your desk in class—reaping the benefits of progressive muscle relaxation without feeling like you're making a big show.

There may be other muscles of yours that tend to tense up during anger or anxiety that you noticed during your first body scan activity. You can target these the same way, purposefully overtightening the area and then letting it relax.

## Tapping

Using the middle and ring fingers of both hands, gently tap where your eyebrows meet your nose. Don't worry about counting out the taps. Gently move your taps up and over your eyebrows, down to the outside corners of your eyes, and then softly under your eyes, spending a little extra time on each of these points before moving to the next. Move your taps down below your nose, then your chin, and then your chest, right where your ribs meet in the middle. You can also try making a fist and rubbing at this area and see what feels better for your body. Finally, reach each set of fingers across your body to tap beneath your opposite underarm (yes, you'll look a bit like a monkey), and then tap the pinky side of one hand, and the pinky side of the other hand.

Move through this pattern a few more times, starting again with your inner eyebrows. Feel free to spend more time in some areas or less time in others, depending on what feels relaxing and calming for your body. It can also help to pair this gentle tapping with a mantra, something you say to yourself to help your brain feel centered. You might repeat the phrase "I'm calm," or "I'm strong," or "I can handle this." You can try out these three, and any others that come to mind, until you find one that really clicks with you.

# MEDITATION AND MINDFULNESS ACTIVITIES

Meditation and mindfulness help our brains quiet down all the noise. Anxious minds tend to have a lot of chatter going on, like, "What's going on? What's coming up next? And, oh my gosh, can you believe what those people just did to me? How dare they? Oh right, what am I supposed to be paying attention to again?"

While we can't stop these thoughts from happening, we can find a way to make them softer, and even let them go. Meditation is the practice of letting thoughts get quiet. Mindfulness is a component of quieting our thoughts that involves tuning in a bit more to something besides our thoughts, like our physical body and the sensations around us. These meditation and mindfulness activities are particularly helpful for teens who feel like their brain is always interrupting them with something else.

*✳ You may be pretty low on your stress elevator with all the previous activities, but make sure you're catching any remaining stress with these meditation and mindfulness activities. ✳*

## Five Senses Grounding Activity

Senses have a way of fading into the background when our brains are focused on the millions of things going on at once. We often tune things out.

This activity helps us ground our physical body and focus on the here and now, rather than on everything else we're feeling stressed, anxious, or angry about.

Wherever you are, I want you to find one thing to look at. There are probably lots of lovely and interesting things to see, but don't look at all of them! Just find one thing to focus your attention on.

Notice the color and how the light hits it. As you look closer, pay attention to all the different shades of color you can see in it. Notice if it seems like it might feel smooth or rough or bumpy.

Next, notice just one thing you hear. Focus on the sound. It may be easier to do this with your eyes closed. Gently notice the tone. Notice if the sound changes at all as you focus more intently.

Notice how the space smells. What scents can you pick up?

Wherever your hands are, notice the texture of what they feel. Notice any temperature differences.

Notice how your mouth tastes.

Notice how you feel in your heart.

Pause.

When you're ready, take a big breath in through your nose, and let it out through your mouth, then slowly reawaken your body to the rest of your surroundings.

## Paper Boats Meditation

Many people think that meditation is all about emptying your mind. Meditate and let your mind go blank. And that's wonderful, if you can totally quiet your mind, but it's honestly basically impossible to do. Even Buddhist monks, the most Zen people out there, talk about our monkey minds. Our brains are always grabbing for the next thought and the next and the next. It's a normal process. It's our brain just doing what it was built to do—and it's okay when thoughts try to interrupt us.

In this exercise, we're going to let any thoughts come up, without judgment. Rather than allowing those thoughts to pick us up with them and get in the way of this meditation, we're going to gently let them go.

Once you've read through this script, I want you to try this meditation with your eyes closed, as it helps filter out distractions that our brains are *designed* to notice and focus on.

Imagine yourself standing in front of a calm, quiet lake. Whenever a thought comes up for you, imagine taking that thought, placing that thought on a paper boat, placing that boat on the water, and letting that boat gently float away.

Sometimes we notice thoughts about what's coming up next or what we have to do. As soon as you notice this thought—or any kind of thought at all—take it, place it on a paper boat, place the boat on the water, and let it gently float away.

We might notice a chain of thoughts, where one thought leads to another and another and another. As soon as you notice this chain of thoughts, take each thought, place each thought on its own paper boat, place each boat gently on the water, and let each boat gently float away.

We might also find that we get caught up in some thoughts, or that some thoughts feel a little sticky. But each time you notice a thought, even if it's the same thought again, just gently take the thought, place the thought on a paper boat, place the boat on the water, and let the boat gently float away. You can do this as many times as you need to.

When you're ready to practice this meditation on your own, set your timer for five minutes and close your eyes. At first, you may notice thoughts like, "What are all these sounds going on around me?" or "My back feels really sore." You might also notice a thought like, "How much longer do I have to do this?"

Remember that for any thought that comes up, you can take that thought, place that thought on a paper boat, place that boat in the water, and let the thought gently float away.

As you practice this meditation the first time, you might notice that your thoughts seem to slow down or quiet as you get further along in your five minutes. The more regularly you practice this meditation, the easier it will be to slip into this quieter state. Remember, though, that your thoughts are impacted by the stressors around you, so if you have a rough day, or something upsetting happens to you, it's okay if this meditation feels less successful and your brain seems so much louder. Remember that we always approach our thoughts without judgment. Fighting against them or trying to ignore them can make them feel bigger. Gently letting them go, as many times as we need, is the best bet.

## Warm Light Guided Meditation

This meditation combines all three clusters of relaxation. Your breathing will slow, your muscles will relax, and your mind will quiet as it focuses on the image. As with the paper boats meditation, read through the script, and then close your eyes. Or bring a friend or a parent into the mix and take turns reading the script for one another. Share the coping skills love!

To allow all your muscles to soften and relax, this meditation works best when you're lying down. Try propping up your head and your legs, right underneath the knees, with soft pillows. You can roll a small blanket into a snake the length of your spine, and place it underneath you, allowing your head to gently drop off. Some people feel more comfortable if they have a blanket or pillow on top of their stomach. Try lying down with a bunch of different props until you find your optimal position, one where you're able to let all your muscles soften and sink into your bed.

Once you've read through these instructions and are ready to begin, close your eyes. Start focusing on your breath. Gently let your breath travel, slowly in through your nose and out through your mouth. Take two more slow, deep breaths, gently in...and out. One more, in...and out. Let your breathing return to its normal resting rate.

Imagine a warm, gentle light floating around your head. Notice its color. Maybe it's your favorite color. Maybe it looks sparkly or see-through or wispy. However it looks to you, you know that when you gaze at it you feel calm and at peace.

With each breath in, imagine that light traveling into your body. Imagine it filling your head, gently swirling around, warming and softening all the muscles in your face. Let that warm light loosen the muscles in your eyebrows, and your jaw, and even let your tongue release from the roof of your mouth.

As you breathe deeper, that warm light slowly fills your body, starting to travel to your neck and letting your neck relax. Then traveling across your shoulders, letting your shoulders soften and sink.

Imagine that warm light slowly, gently flowing down across your back, softening all the tendons along your vertebrae, swirling around any areas of your back where you notice stress and tension, and letting those places warm and ease.

From your shoulders, imagine that warm light filling your upper arms, your elbows, your forearms, and flowing into the palms of your hands and each finger, one by one.

From the base of your throat, let that warm, gentle light travel down to your heart, letting it radiate from your heart across your chest and into your belly, letting all the muscles around your belly soften and smooth out.

With your next breath in and out, the warm light travels down your legs, into your knees, across your calves and shins, until it fills your feet and each toe.

As your muscles relax and the warm light travels around your body, notice any other tension that you want to send the light to. You may notice a buzzing sensation, or an urge to move, but just let your muscles be still and relax, staying here for a few moments.

When you're ready to finish your meditation, remember that you can come back to this relaxed space whenever you need to. Notice how that warm light helps you to bring gratitude to yourself, in your heart, for taking the time to relax.

Gently move your fingers and your toes, reintroducing small movements into your body. You'll end this meditation with three deep breaths, breathing in through your nose, and sighing out through your mouth. With your third deep breath, gently open your eyes, and slowly sit yourself all the way back up.

## CONSIDERATIONS FOR RELAXATION ACTIVITIES

Evaluate your stress elevator. What activities moved you down your stress elevator the most? Which ones seemed less effective for you?

Some people feel worse after certain relaxation activities, noticing that their stress level has elevated after some activities. This can be due to a myriad of reasons—remember, everybody is different—but if this happens, no need to worry that something is wrong with you.

One teen I worked with really hated using any of the breathing activities. Every time we would try one, she reported an increase in her heart rate and muscle tension. She could have avoided any future relaxation work I suggested, but instead, she was open to trying lots of different strategies (and kudos to her for trying something important, even though it felt hard and uncomfortable).

When we experience anxiety, especially anxiety-driven anger, our brain at some level is telling us that we're in danger and we need to protect ourselves. Your brain might be telling you to protect yourself against something specific, like a test or a person or a situation, or you may have the kind of anxiety where you just feel like you need to be on guard all the time. We sometimes experience nameless fears. We feel nervous, but there's no real reason why.

If your body is nervous, and your brain is telling you to be aware of danger, of course it's going to feel uncomfortable to practice a coping skill. Your brain doesn't like relaxing, because feeling relaxed means you're no longer in that guarded, protective mode. We especially find this in people who have experienced big stressors or even trauma.

For this teen, we found that it was easier to start with muscle relaxation activities, and once she could reach a certain level of calm, we could move on to a meditation in the same session. We also incorporated mantras to help remind her brain that she was in a calm, safe space, and that it was okay to relax. Eventually, through cognitive behavioral therapy, we were able to use breathing activities without causing an anxiety spike. By the end of our time together, these activities still weren't her go-to, but she could use them without causing any stress increase.

It's okay if any of these skills seemed ineffective, or even made your stress elevator get higher. Take some time to figure out why that may have happened. What about the skills felt less effective for you?

Let's also explore which activities felt most helpful for you. Which ones did you like the best? Which ones helped you calm the most?

As you think about your typical day, figure out which coping skills are going to be the ones you want to start regularly adding to your life, and which coping skills are going to be your go-to's in the moment when you notice an increase in your anxiety, stress, or anger. Write down your plan for regular relaxation practice. You can even schedule it into your phone's calendar, so you know when it's going to happen.

Remember that regular relaxation practice is like releasing the stress built up from your dam. Releasing that water before you get to a crisis point means you can handle more stress overall. And when you're coping with your stress, and building in relaxation throughout your week, you'll notice that your anger, anxiety, and stress levels are within a much more manageable range. You'll probably feel more at ease and less likely to snap. You'll handle annoying things that come your way. You'll make better choices. You won't be so overwhelmed. Eventually, you'll feel in charge of your emotions instead of your emotions being in charge of you. And you're going to feel so proud of yourself when you reach that point.

# CHAPTER 6

# Problem Solving with Anxiety-Driven Anger

We come across problems every single day. Some problems seem huge, and some seem pretty small. Some problems are so tiny, we can barely remember them the next day. So, why is it that we can feel so stuck when we get to a problem and don't know what to do? What makes problems hard to solve? What's the difference between a problem we barely remember the next day, and a problem so all-consuming that we can't even focus on anything else?

A big piece of why some problems can be so hard to deal with is any anxiety-driven anger you experience. Anxiety-driven anger gets in the way of problem solving because it (1) makes it too hard to think about the problem and (2) makes us ineffective problem solvers. It impacts how we feel and think internally, and it impacts the behaviors we present externally.

You may have noticed something like this happening to you before. A problem occurs, like your girlfriend getting mad at you for flirting with another girl, and she's *so wrong* about what happened that it's hard for you to even talk to her and defend yourself. You feel really anxious because she's blaming you for something you didn't do, and you feel really upset that she would even think that you'd flirt with someone else. Your anxiety-driven anger means that you get too flooded to think clearly—and when trying to explain yourself, you start shouting, which means your girlfriend just thinks you're more guilty. You're too caught up in that angry/anxious combo to be able to calmly explain yourself, ask what you both could do differently next time, and actually move forward. You have a huge argument instead of solving the problem.

To solve a problem, you need to understand it, so let's figure it out. What makes problem solving a problem for you?

## WHAT ARE YOU REALLY IN CHARGE OF?

One of the biggest reasons that problems feel so difficult is because we have a fundamental misunderstanding about how much we can impact. Things would be so much easier if we were always in control, right? If we always had things go our way. If we always got what we wanted.

Even if that were to happen (and honestly, it sounds a little exhausting to me to always be in control), it's impossible. There's only so much we can do. There's only so much we're really responsible for. You are not in control of everything that happens to you.

## WHO'S THE BOSS?

Have you ever had a boss? Even if you haven't, you certainly have adults who tell you what to do. You have people in your life who are in charge of you. But we need to be really clear about this distinction: in charge is not the same thing as in control.

Let's pretend you work at a fancy pizzeria. Your boss tells you to take the pizzas out of the wood-fired oven. Is your boss in control of you? No. You could decide to keep those pizzas in the oven, and even let them burn, though of course you might get in trouble, or even get fired for insubordination. Your boss doesn't control your actions, even when they're the one in charge.

Now let's say you choose to not take the pizzas out. You decide, for whatever reason, to let them burn. Your boss gets upset and shouts at you. You probably wish your boss would stop shouting. Are you in control of your boss shouting? Nope. Are you even in charge of your boss shouting? No, again. Your boss is the one in charge, both of themself and, in their role as boss, of you, their employee, even though they couldn't control your decision to burn the pizzas.

Because your boss is shouting at you about the burnt food, you find yourself shouting right back at them. You don't feel like you're in control of your reactions. Are you in charge of your reaction? Yep, but sometimes, our emotional outbursts are happening outside of our control. We can be the boss of our emotions and our thoughts, but that doesn't always mean our body or our brain is going to follow our directions.

There's a subtle yet crucial difference between "in control" and "in charge." Control doesn't really exist, even when you're talking about trying to control your thoughts or your emotions. However, being in charge means that you're the one steering the ship. As a teenager, there's not a lot that you're in charge of. You're not in charge of other people in your life, even if you'd like to be. You're not in charge of your parents. You're not in charge of what happens to you. The only thing you're in charge of is yourself.

## THE SPHERE OF INFLUENCE

I want you to picture yourself standing in the middle of a circle. This is you. You decide what to say, think, feel, and do, and you're in charge of yourself. Sometimes it might feel like you react more strongly than you'd like to, or you regret things you've done, but you are in charge of you. This circle is the start of your sphere of influence, and obviously you have a lot of influence over yourself.

Visualize drawing a second circle around you, but this one is bigger. In this circle are your family and friends—your close, interpersonal relationships. These people have a lot of influence on you. They impact you by offering feedback on your external actions and can also influence you when you change your behaviors based on your concern around their reactions to you. Your parents can get you in trouble and your friends can shut you down, so that's pretty big. You care about what they think. You modify what you're doing because of them.

Draw a third circle around you, much bigger this time. This circle holds your school, which is the big social institution you're a part of. It would also include any sports or clubs that you're a member of. Your school's rules definitely influence you. They impact what you can and cannot do, unless you want to get in trouble.

Now we'll add a huge fourth circle, made up of your community. Your community also has big rules and regulations that you are influenced by. You have the follow the laws, like waiting to drive until you get your driver's license and not drinking underage. The consequences for breaking these rules would generally be pretty humongous.

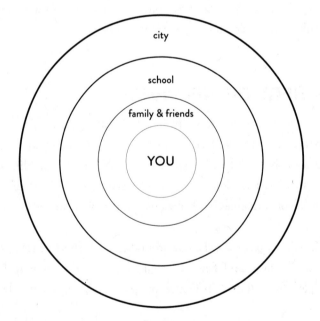

Looking at this sphere of influence, you can see all these layers that impact you: family, friends, school, and community. But what part of this sphere are you in charge of? Ding ding ding, that's right! You're in charge of only that first circle—yourself. Your thoughts, your feelings, your behaviors. You're not in charge of your family or friends. You're not in charge of your school or your community.

Can you influence these other circles around you? Yes. Your influence is just like dropping a pebble in a lake. The water ripples out from that pebble, each new ripple smaller than the first. Your actions and choices can ripple out around you, and you have more influence on those circles closest to you. You can have conversations with your friends and family, talk to teachers, or even write letters to your community leaders.

The impact you have decreases the further out you go, but it's still there. Some people start to feel disheartened when they realize that their sphere of influence is so small, that they're only in charge of that pebble. I think it's liberating. You can be a positive force for change, and you can make those positive decisions ripple out among your friends and family, school, and larger community while simultaneously recognizing that it doesn't all come down to you.

When it comes to problem solving, recognize that you are in charge of you. How you respond ripples out and impacts those spheres of influence, but you're not the one deciding how people are going to respond to you.

## Example: Living in a Pandemic

I started writing this book right before the COVID-19 pandemic, and with each new chapter, the situation progressed. What started as a little problem turned into lockdowns, massive infection rates and casualties, and a huge change to the world we live in.

Teens missed out on high school graduations, in-person college, and so many big and important life events. Over the course of the pandemic, we had to get used to wearing masks and social distancing. For me right now, it's almost hard to remember what life was like before COVID-19. Watching movies and TV shows, it feels strange to see people hugging, shaking hands, or sharing drinks. It's like looking at a different world.

Living during a pandemic, of course, has a huge impact on stress, which makes problem solving even harder.

Picture a student, Becca, attending her virtual English class. She was expected to read five books over her summer vacation, but she just didn't have the energy because, hello, pandemic summer. Her teacher, Mr. Witmer, doesn't know how to work the technology to move the conversation into a separate virtual room, so instead, he talks to Becca while the whole class is signed on and listening in. Mr. Witmer says, "Hey, I understand this summer was hard, Becca, but everyone had to read five books. What's your plan for fixing this?"

Becca feels a spike of anxiety. Not only is her teacher making a big deal about this, he's making it a big deal in front of the whole class. Becca wants to shout at him, "Listen, I just couldn't deal with it, okay?!" Becca doesn't want to explain about her grandpa getting sick and passing away from COVID, her dad losing his job, and the fear she felt whenever she had to leave the house. How could she possibly have completed the summer reading when there was always another catastrophe waiting around the corner?

Becca knows Mr. Witmer expects an answer right away. She doesn't want to get into all the details about why this summer was so hard, so she just says, "Mr. Witmer, I'm sorry. Can we set up a time to talk about this after class?" Mr. Witmer agrees, thank goodness, so Becca has some time to problem solve before their meeting.

As we're gazing in on this problem, we can think about Becca's sphere of influence. There are a whole bunch of problems she can't really fix, even though they're significantly impacting her. On the community level, COVID is happening, and that's obviously a huge stress. School-wise, somehow the teachers expect her to still be participating and doing everything during virtual classes like there's not a global pandemic. Family and friends-wise, Becca's experiencing a lot of added stress following the death of her grandpa and her dad losing his job. She's not in charge of any of these problems.

What is Becca in charge of? Herself—including whether she completed the summer reading.

Between the start of class and checking in with Mr. Witmer, Becca realizes she really doesn't want her grade lowered. Rather than getting upset and defending herself, Becca decides to ask for help. "Mr. Witmer," she says, "this summer was really difficult for me, but I understand that I didn't complete the requirement. I've been really overwhelmed with everything that's going on. Could I maybe do some extra reading this semester to make up for it?"

It's not up to Becca whether her teacher says yes or no. We can provide problem-solving suggestions, but we're not in charge of what others decide to do. All we can do is make our case. So when Mr. Witmer responds, "I appreciate that this summer was hard, and you know, it was really hard for me too. But we have a summer requirement for a reason. I'll let you have partial credit if you can finish up one book and write a report on it by the end of the month," it's not an ideal outcome for her, but it's better than nothing. Becca decides to be okay with it. She'll get through it. She doesn't blow up. She moves forward.

The sphere of influence helps us look at the big picture and recognize that, at times, our role is limited. It can help keep us from getting all worked up, like we might if we felt we could be in control of everything. Instead, it's a clear way to see that we're not in charge of everything, and we can't always get exactly what we want. We can just do our best during situations that happen to us.

## WORK IT OUT OR LET IT GO?

When it comes to dealing with a problem, you always have options. You can work it out or you can just let it go. Letting go means deciding to opt out of the problem. You don't hold on to a grudge or decide to bring the problem up later—you decide to fully move on past the problem at hand.

For example, let's say you're outside for varsity tennis practice. The sun is shining, and there's a gentle breeze in the air. You're excited to be here, which doesn't always happen when it comes time for practice, but you've been really improving at your game, starting to make friends with the other girls on the team, and feeling more confident about yourself. You see a new girl on the team. She's talking on the phone, and you realize she must have just moved here. You walk over to introduce yourself, but as you wait to jump in, you overhear her say, "Everyone at this school is so dumb. I literally hate it here."

Is it important enough to wait until she's done with her conversation, and then defend your school and yourself? Do you really need to jump in and work it out? Or does it make more sense to just let it go and focus on tennis practice?

In this situation, it's probably more important to just let it go and enjoy the rest of practice, so you do. Who knows what's going on with her day? We could put ourselves in her shoes—maybe she's had a rough day at her new school. Maybe she's being defensive. Maybe she's always like this. The thing is, it doesn't have to matter to you. The sun is still out. The breeze is still nice. You can still enjoy the rest of practice today.

Deciding to let it go means not picking up the problem later. You're not going to wait until the end of practice and then tell your new teammate you overheard her conversation and need to talk. It also doesn't mean you're going to hold it against her. It's a classic "oh well" scenario—you may not like what she said, but it's not worth spending your time or energy on it. You fully shrug it off.

Everyone has different triggers for their anxiety-driven anger, which means that what feels easy for you to let go of, and what doesn't, is entirely personal. You may decide that it does make sense for you to work this out instead of letting it go, because you're really motivated to be friends with your teammate, and this is 100 percent going to negatively impact your relationship. You may find that you have no problem letting it go when it's something related to friendships, but you almost always want to work out a problem that impacts your grades or your schoolwork. Maybe you don't mind problems when they're small, but you always want to work one out when it feels like a big problem. Or the reverse could be true—it's easier for you to let something go when it is so big picture, but you like working out the small stuff before it grows.

You always have a choice between letting it go or working it out. If you decide to work out a problem instead of letting it go, that's a totally valid option. Working it out is different from making a problem bigger. It's calmly collecting yourself, exploring the problem, coming up with some potential solutions, and then moving forward with that solution or going back to the drawing board with some feedback.

You're probably used to adults coming up with silly acronyms to help you remember things. You might use some acronyms yourself when you're studying for a test and trying to remember a particular list of items. Luckily for you, I have the *best* acronym there is to remember the steps. This acronym actually is SILLY.

**S**    Stay calm

**I**    Investigate the problem

**L**    Look for solutions

**L**    Listen to feedback

**Y**    Yes or no (and back to the drawing board)

SILLY can take some time to implement, because you need to have a calm attitude, brainstorm ideas, propose a potential solution, and follow up until you have a good plan for moving forward. When your body is used to getting really upset when faced with a problem, using SILLY can be a real challenge. That's why, as with all the other tools in this book, it's important to practice using it before you really need it. The more often you practice a skill, the easier it is to use.

Here's SILLY in action:

You're getting ready to head out to a Friday night party at your best friend Marcus's house. You've been helping him plan for a couple of weeks, down to coming up with the perfect playlist. You've figured out your cutest outfit and even got a haircut the week before so that it's just the right amount of grown out. You are so excited.

To be honest, you've been so excited about this party that you've kind of put your homework on the back burner. When you ask your dad for the keys to the car, he says, "Wait a minute. I know you've got your big party tonight, but I just got an email from your physics teacher. You've turned in your past two assignments late, and you didn't turn in the paper that was due today. What gives?"

You quickly try to explain. "I know, I know, but I told Mrs. Fitzley that I would turn it in on Monday and she said it was okay!"

Your dad responds, "I'm glad you talked with your teacher, but I'm concerned. You need to work on your paper, and I don't think you should go to the party until it's finished."

You know what it's a perfect time for? SILLY.

## S: Stay calm

When your dad tells you that you should stay home, you automatically notice two big emotions: frustration and, underneath it, anxiety. You're worried that he won't let you go. You're also stressed because you did figure out a solution with Mrs. Fitzley, and now your dad is saying that the solution isn't good enough.

Rather than having those emotions spill out, you remember how important it is to stay calm. You squeeze your fists really, really tight for four counts, and then let them relax, wiggling your fingers. Then you tighten your forearms for four counts and relax for four. Next, you bring your shoulders up to your ears for four counts, and then relax and drop them down. Finally, you gently tilt your head to one side and the other, stretching out your neck. You feel much calmer.

## I: Investigate the problem

Your next step is to investigate the problem, figuring out your dad's perspective compared to yours, so that everyone is on the same page about what's going on. We can't just go off on our assumptions, like thinking your dad doesn't trust you. It might be something else, and it's important to take the time to listen to someone's viewpoint rather than just focusing on making yourself heard.

Making sure that your tone matches your calmer emotional state, you ask your dad, "If Mrs. Fitzley is okay with me turning it in on Monday, why do you need me to work on it tonight when I have the whole weekend?" You see your dad start to get a look on his face, like parents can do when their kid asks them to defend their decisions (yep, parents would probably benefit from this book, too!). Experience has taught you that your dad can get frustrated when you question his decisions, so you quickly add, "I'm really open to your feedback, Dad. I just want to make sure I understand your concerns so I can address them for you."

Your dad responds, "I'm glad you talked with your teacher about it, but I don't think you realize that you're not going to have enough time this weekend to finish your paper to the level we expect. You've got soccer games on Saturday and Sunday, plus our family cookout at your grandparents' house on Sunday night."

Remembering to clarify and ensure you both understand the identified problem, you say, "Okay, you're worried that I'm not going to complete it because this is a busy weekend, and I have lots of stuff going on between now and Monday. Right?"

"Right."

## L: Look for solutions

Time to propose some potential solutions, remembering that this may just be your first run-through. You know you really, really want to get to this party tonight, and you also know that your dad thinks it would be better for you to work on your paper tonight rather than trying to get the whole thing finished this weekend.

You suggest, "What if, instead of working on it tonight, I get up early Saturday and Sunday before my games?"

## L: Listen to feedback

Your dad responds, "You're actually going to get up before eleven on the weekend? That never happens."

You laugh. "I know, I know, I do love my sleep. But I seriously will get up early this weekend, and I'll make sure I don't stay out too late tonight."

"I mean, that's great if it works out, but is the morning really going to give you enough time? I still think you should get started on it tonight."

You incorporate the feedback into your next proposal. "I hear you. I do think getting up early will give me enough time, but what about if I bring my computer to Grandma's on Sunday, too, if I need it? I'll work in their computer room if I'm not at a good enough spot to turn in the paper Monday."

## Y: Yes or no (and back to the drawing board)

You wait as your dad weighs the pros and cons. Is he going to let you go? Is Marcus going to have to host the party without you? Is everyone going to have an awesome time while you totally miss out?

You take a deep breath in through your nose and let it out through your mouth, and you remember that you're not in charge of what your dad decides; you're just in charge of what you say and how you react.

Your dad lifts his head, raises his eyebrows, and peers at you through half-closed eyes. Ah yes, his skeptical face. This could go either way.

"If you really think you'll get it done, and you don't mind missing out on Grandma's cookout with the family, then okay. You can head out tonight."

Yes!

Now that we understand how to implement SILLY, let's go through some examples and you can decide whether you'd rather let it go or work it out. Remember, this is a totally personal decision, and both options can be good. It all comes down to what seems like the best fit for you and your needs.

- You've been waiting all week after tryouts to see what role you got in the school play. Your friend helped with casting and hasn't said a word, even though you've asked her repeatedly if you got the lead. You find out that the director has posted the play assignments on the choir room door. You hurry down and see...you're in the chorus. You're not even a named character; you're Townsperson #3. You feel upset with your friend for not at least giving you a heads-up. Do you want to let it go or work it out?

- You're standing in line for lunch. You're starving. You were late getting here, so you only have fifteen minutes to eat before your next period, and you need to speed it up. Just as you're getting close to checking out, a group of girls walks right in front of you, cutting the line. Is this a big problem or a small problem? A work-it-out problem or a let-it-go problem?

- You turn in your history paper feeling pretty hopeful about the grade, but when you get it back your teacher has graded it a C−. He left corrections in red all over it. In his comments, he noted that you didn't correctly complete the assignment. You talked one-on-one with him about it after class last week, so you're surprised. Should you let it go or work it out?

- You're playing an online video game with some friends. You're pumped because you've been doing a lot of research on how to beat this particular level. You go through the moves and solve the puzzles, and your friend says, "Ummm, wow, I didn't think you were that smart." This annoys you. What do you think is best? Work it out? Let it go?

- You have a big assignment due tomorrow, and you've been putting it off because it feels too overwhelming. Of course, now that it's the night before, it somehow, magically, feels even more overwhelming. Who would have thought? Anyway, you tell your mom you're feeling stressed out about it and need some help. Your mom says, "Sorry, I'm busy. I could have helped yesterday, but you waited till the last minute again. Maybe you'll learn something from this for next time." Do you want to work this out with your mom? Or do you want to let this go?

These scenarios may have started turning some wheels in your brain. Think through one or two problems that you've recently faced. In each of those situations, would it have been better to let it go or work it out? How does this decision inform your choice for the next problem you face? What would you like to do the same next time? What would you like to do differently?

## WHAT GETS IN YOUR WAY?

Letting it go or working it out are both fantastic options when it comes to solving problems, because you get to decide if you want to solve it or if it doesn't really need to be solved. Problem solving works externally, with others, and internally, with yourself. You can bring people into the fold and co-create a plan for moving forward, or you can deal with the problems internally by letting them go.

Sometimes there are obstacles that make it difficult to problem solve effectively, and they can even make you give up on the whole endeavor. Here are your obstacle ABCs: assumptions, blame, and control.

Assumptions—What's that saying about assumptions and you and me? Hmm... Okay, here's the thing about assumptions. When you assume something, without taking the time to gather the facts or double-check your opinion, you may be making a *false* assumption—assuming certain information is true when it's actually not. You might also assume that there are certain obstacles in the way that would prevent potential solutions. Or you might assume that there's a different background to the problem, which keeps you from letting it go. We need to gather all the data that we can, and even question our assumptions, to get a really full picture of all the options available to us.

Blame—It's much more difficult to problem solve·when you are assigning blame, especially if you're not open to taking some of that blame for yourself. Even if you know the problem is occurring because of x, y, and z external factors, you need to be able to take some personal responsibility. Separately, if you're entirely fixated on who is at fault, you're going to get distracted from your main goal, which is getting through the problem—not figuring out who caused what. Blame is really fixated on figuring out who is at fault. What if everyone is? What if no one is?

Control—While we've discussed your sphere of influence, and you understand what you're actually in charge of, control is still going to rear its head from time to time. Especially with your anxiety-driven anger, you're still going to want to try to control situations and certain outcomes. It's just a matter of fact. When you're having trouble letting go of a problem, or using SILLY, take a step back to see if that need for control is playing a role.

It's good to check in on your ABCs if you're having difficulty problem solving. These are the big three to check in with. Other problems may be getting in your way, too, like people not being open to your solutions, or getting into a rut where the same type of problem keeps coming up over and over again.

## MOVING ON TO BUILD RESILIENCE

The biggest key to problem solving is recognizing that it takes time, and it doesn't always work. You can't solve every problem. What you can do is feel better about the problems that come your way. You can keep yourself from exploding. You can move forward from more and more things. You can let more stuff go. You can be willing to try and solve your problems, each time, and you can be gentle with yourself when it doesn't work out as planned.

There's never going to be a magic wand. There's never going to be a perfect solution. You're never going to stop having problems. You will always have challenges. This is part of being human!

Instead of feeling overwhelmed by the fact that you'll always face problems, embrace it. Dealing with problems makes you a stronger person. Each time you face what's going on, you build your resilience, and you make it easier to face any new difficulties that come your way. You get better at dealing with things. You don't let your anxiety-driven anger tell you that you can't handle things, or that the only way to respond is a big explosive reaction. You are empowered to make your own choices. You can deal with problems. You can move forward and decide that it's just time to move on.

# CHAPTER 7

# The Three-Step Approach to Anxiety and Anger Management

To bake a cake, you need a recipe, and that's what this chapter is all about. Not actually a recipe for some baked goods (though I may sneak one in below), but a formula you can follow to get the kind of outcome you want. I'm going to share with you the recipe for managing anxiety-driven anger.

When you're baking, you get a chance to put your own spin on it too, once you're confident enough in your skills. I don't know if you ever read cooking blogs or watch baking videos, but the comments sections are usually filled with people saying, "I replaced the sour cream with cream cheese and somehow it didn't work," or "I know you said to use plain flour, but I used potato flour, and these biscuits were DISGUSTING—DO. NOT. MAKE." You can't totally substitute something for something else unless you understand how the recipe works, and what components create what results. My grandma always says you should do a recipe run-through. Follow the recipe, exactly as written, and then tweak from there.

In our previous chapters, you've learned some important rules of baking. You've learned how to identify what you're feeling, what you're thinking, and how to problem solve. Just like watching your grandma bake a cake as a kid and practicing measuring out the ingredients with her, stirring the batter, and putting the whole thing into the oven. Your grandma would step in to make sure things were done according to plan, and she probably didn't let little five-year-old you reach into the oven on your own. She was there to guide you and help you and watch over you, stepping in when needed. Now you're a little older and a little wiser, and you're ready to start doing this whole baking thing a little more on your own.

Our plan in Chapter 7 is to pull your basic skills together and figure out how to do this whole anger/anxiety management thing on your own. Below is the recipe for managing your anxiety-driven anger. Run through it, and then get ready to tweak it as needed, based on your specific situations. Once you've done it in a few situations, you'll be more ready to substitute in your ingredients as needed, and tailor the recipe to your needs. Let's get cooking!

(Okay, and here's the best brownies recipe ever: Preheat your oven to 350° F. Melt 8 tablespoons of butter and mix with 1 cup of sugar and ¾ cup of cocoa powder. Whisk in 2 eggs, one at a time, 1 teaspoon of vanilla, a small pinch of salt, and ½ cup of flour. Then, butter an 8 by 8 pan and line with parchment paper. Pour the batter into the pan and bake until a toothpick comes out with just a few crumbs sticking to it, about 20 minutes. Enjoy!)

## THE THREE-STEP APPROACH

Problems can be internal or external. Internal problems are ones you're facing with yourself, such as being upset that you're upset, or not liking how you react to certain situations. You can have a problem with how you feel, how you look, how you react, how you think, and so on. Almost everyone can be self-critical at times.

External problems are ones that are happening outside yourself. These are problems about the people, places, and situations that are happening outside of your control, like getting a flat tire on your way to football practice, which then makes you late.

Many problems are a combination of these two sets. You have an external stressor happening outside yourself, and your internal stressor happening within.

Throughout this book, we've been practicing acceptance of our thoughts, feelings, and behaviors, and of the world around us. We accept that thoughts can come up any time they want to. Struggling against them doesn't work as well as just noticing them and being okay with them. We've also been practicing how to accept our emotions, like recognizing that anger is useful, and that anxiety is trying to keep us safe. Even when we don't like the physical experiences of those emotions or how our bodies display those feelings, we can accept that they need to happen from time to time. Finally, we accept that problems happen, that we're not in control of anything, and that there are certain things that can happen to us, no matter how much we dislike them.

When you're dealing with problems, whether they're internal, external, or both, there's a simple, three-step approach that will guide you through any overwhelming situation. You have to first tune in and calm down, and then you can move forward when you're ready.

**Step 1—Identify and empathize.** What am I feeling? What's going on? What emotion do I first notice? (Anger?) What else is coming up for me? (Stress, anxiety, worry?)

Way back in Chapter 1, we completed a body clues activity where we explored your physical experience of emotions. Emotions live in different parts of our body, and sometimes overlap in terms of where we experience them. Our wires can get crossed about what we're feeling and why. That's why it's so crucial to identify what you're feeling, *and* to give yourself enough space to correct that first identification. "Yes, I feel mad…and sitting with it for a bit, I also feel hurt." Or "Obviously I'm so upset! I feel totally betrayed! I'm also a little relieved that I don't have to go do this thing anymore." The first emotion you notice isn't always the full picture, which is why you need to tune in to what else might be going on in your feelings.

Whatever you're feeling, practice being okay with it. Notice the feeling nonjudgmentally. We want to empathize with ourselves. You'll practice telling yourself things like, "It's okay to feel this way," or "It makes sense to be upset right now," or "I can feel this, and it doesn't have to feel too big if I don't need it to."

Your goal with this step is to notice and explore your emotions, without pushing them away. Being nonjudgmental about your feelings is key. *Pathologizing* the feeling—treating it as abnormal and unhealthy—makes it hard to solve the external problem and move past it, because you get focused on what you're doing wrong, and how what you're feeling is wrong.

**Step 2—Calm down.** Whatever you're feeling, you want to lower the temperature before you try to solve the problem. If you're flooded, or high up on your emotions elevator, you won't be able to think very clearly. Calming down your body helps you calm down your brain.

In Chapter 5, you developed some coping skills that will be really useful for calming yourself. We can categorize your relaxation options under three umbrellas: breathing skills, muscle skills, and mindfulness and meditation skills. You may want to call upon different skills depending on the type of overwhelming situation you find yourself in. Some situations may allow you to set aside ten minutes for a guided meditation; in other situations, you may just have a few moments to take some heart and belly breaths. You have probably already identified a couple of go-to's that really click with your body and brain, but that doesn't keep you from adding to your toolbox. Be open to trying new skills as you're exposed to them, and remember that practicing a skill before you need it makes it much, much easier to call upon it when you're in the middle of a problem—like when you're in the middle of this three-step approach.

It can also be a good idea to stack up multiple relaxation strategies to really impact you and bring you down on your window of tolerance. Just one skill may not cut it in the moment. You may need to take a deep breath *and* do a five-senses grounding activity, *and* also tense and relax some muscles, to really curb your trajectory and keep you within your window.

Use as many skills as you need to calm down enough to think, and you're always welcome to take a break in the middle of the problem until you're calm enough. Note that we say "enough." You don't have to be totally chilled out to solve the problem. You just have to be calm enough to move forward.

**Step 3—Come up with a game plan.** All right, you've identified what you're feeling, and you've calmed down enough to think. Now it's time to come up with your game plan and solve the problem as best you can. This is the step where you ask yourself, "What can I do next?" Game planning is very situation-specific, so it's good to have a few general guidelines that you tailor to what's happening for you.

Generally, it's helpful to start from a place of acknowledging that the situation stinks, and that you probably wish you weren't in it. Even though it stinks, what's the best possible outcome? What's the next best? What's the third best? Acknowledge what's likely and doable, and be okay with the fact that this may be less than ideal.

Once you have figured out your goal in this situation, like the specific outcomes you'd like to reach, break your goal down into steps. Find out what you can do to solve the problem and get as close as possible to your ideal result.

## Running Through the Recipe

Remember, you want to try out the recipe and get comfortable with it before tweaking it to really suit your needs, and the more you practice, the easier it is to figure out what you can change and when. So now that we have our three-step approach, let's walk through an example of how to use it.

Jayden was starting his first day at his new high school. His family had just moved over the summer, and he didn't know anyone in his new town. He got a little lost on his way to his first class, so he got there five minutes after the bell. His teacher, Mr. Knox, was in the middle of explaining the course outline for the semester. "You're late," he said, "and I won't tolerate that moving forward. Sit down. Now." He pointed to an empty desk.

When Jayden walked over to his desk, he accidentally dropped his half-zipped book bag and all the books fell out. His new classmates started giggling, and Mr. Knox seemed to glare at his over his glasses. Jayden decided, right then and there, that he hated his new school, his classmates, and especially Mr. Knox. As soon as the bell rang, he jumped up from his chair, ran to the court-yard, and called his mom. Before his mom had even finished saying, "Hello?" Jada shouted, "I hate this school! I hate you! I hate everything about moving! I've had the worst day already, and I'm dropping Mr. Knox's class—I don't care what you have to say about it!"

**Step 1: Identify and empathize.** Obviously, Jayden's feeling pretty angry, but what else might he be feeling underneath that? Let's walk backward through this chain of events. He seems angry with his mom about the move, and angry with Mr. Knox and his classmates. Underneath that anger, he may have felt embarrassed about dropping his books and being late, and before that, he probably was feeling sad or lonely about the move. Could he have also been feeling anxious about being in a new school and in a new town? Does it make sense to feel anxiety when you get blamed for something that you didn't do on purpose?

The answer is, of course it makes sense! Even if Jayden was just feeling angry, that would be okay, but there's a lot swirling inside besides anger.

**Step 2: Calm down.** You may have noticed a few points where Jayden could have used some coping skills. He could have checked in with his stress levels while trying to find the classroom and taken a few deep breaths to calm down and make it easier to find his class. After he dropped his books, Jayden could have felt that embarrassment and anxiety and used a mini progressive muscle relaxation, focusing on squeezing lemons and tensing and relaxing his shoulders. Before even getting to school, Jayden could have started his day with a guided meditation in the car, to help him relax and start his day off on a calmer foot.

Sometimes, though, we're not able to check in with ourselves until after a whole big event has occurred. Let's say that Jayden felt too flooded in his classroom to use coping skills but was able to check in with herself by the time he called his mom. Before he dials his mom, he notices his hurt, anger, frustration, anxiety, and sadness all swirling around, and decides to ground himself by placing one hand on his heart and slowly breathing in through his nose and out through his mouth. He feels the sun on his face, smells the breeze, and notices his heart beating as it slows down. His muscles loosen. He's ready for step 3.

**Step 3: Come up with a game plan.** We don't have to solve every problem on our own. It can be helpful to get feedback from a supportive person, like a parent. In this situation, Jayden has calmed down enough to call his mom, and he really wants his mother's feedback. Jayden and his mom have a healthy relationship, and Jayden feels like he can trust his mom to be open and honest. You may have a different point person, like a close teacher, guidance counselor, or a friend who always gives good advice, and that's all right.

Jayden thinks about how he would like to solve the problem—he still wants to drop Mr. Knox's class—and talks his solution through with his mom. "Mom, you won't believe what just happened. I was late to class and accidentally made this huge, embarrassing mess, and I think my teacher hates me. There's no way I'm going back there. Can I just switch to a different class and teacher for this period?"

Jayden's mom responds, "Honey, I hear you, and I'm so sorry that happened. I don't think it's a good idea to drop the class, though. You need the credits, and I don't want you to have to move your whole schedule around just because you want a different teacher. What if you talked to Mr. Knox at the end of school today to explain what happened?"

Jayden's not too thrilled about that idea, so he offers a compromise. "Okay, I won't drop the class, but I don't want to talk to Mr. Knox today. Maybe I can see if it gets any more comfortable for me this week? But if he still seems mean, or if I feel like he's being really strict and picking on me, can you be open to me trying out a different teacher for this period?"

Jayden's mom agrees, and Jayden is able to get a version of the outcome he'd really like. He does his best to keep an open mind for the rest of the week, and by Friday he decides that he'd rather not deal with Mr. Knox at all. It's worth the effort to move all his classes around to get a new teacher for that class period, and his parents help his out because they want his to feel more comfortable at his new school.

Your game plan may look totally different from Jayden's, but that's the beauty of our three-step approach—you get to figure out what works best for you.

Now it's your turn. Think of a recent situation that led to an overwhelming amount of anxiety or anxiety-driven anger for you. Maybe you can even think of a situation that you're experiencing remorse about, or a time where you wish you had reacted in a different way, but your judgment was clouded by how much you didn't like what was going on. Grab some paper, or open your Notes app on your phone, and answer the following questions in order:

- What happened that prompted your emotional reaction? Jot down a few details before you move on. (When we remember a situation from the past, it's helpful to add in details and think about who was involved, what occurred, where and when it happened, and why you were upset.)

- **Step 1: Identify and empathize.** (No matter what you were feeling, it's okay, and it's also okay to calm down.)

   What were you feeling in the moment?

   As you put yourself back in that space, what other emotions do you notice coming up in your body?

   Remembering your anger iceberg, were there any emotions bubbling up underneath the surface?

   Is it okay to have those feelings?

   What can you tell yourself about the feelings you experienced that's helpful and accepting?

- **Step 2: Calm down.**

   In that moment, what would have been a good relaxation strategy?

   Do you think it would have been easy to use that relaxation strategy? Would you have needed to use a few different tools?

   How would you have known you were calm enough to move on to the next step?

- **Step 3: Come up with a game plan.**

   What outcome would you have wanted from this situation? What would have been a good enough version of that?

   What steps could you have taken to reach that outcome?

   What could you have proposed to anyone in that situation to move forward from that problem?

   What responsibility could you have taken in that situation? What were you in charge of? What weren't you in charge of?

   Even if nothing else changed in the situation, how could you have still moved forward from it?

## Troubleshooting

Let's say you're making crème brûlée for the very first time. You've made awesome chocolate pudding before, and it seems like the process for this fancy French custard would be similar. You follow the recipe exactly as written, but you end up with a soggy mess of half-scrambled eggs rather than a smooth, rich, velvety custard.

Does this automatically mean you should never attempt crème brûlée again? No, of course not. Does this mean that you're a bad cook? No again. Crème brûlée troubles are due to the recipe being more challenging and labor intensive. It calls for a new skill set.

You have the components needed to manage problems in your life, but even when you have a great recipe, you need to be able to figure out what could go wrong. With that in mind, we're going to talk about what can get in the way of these three steps. We want to know what to do to fix the soggy mess, or to at least get back on track for next time.

**Step 1: Identify and empathize.** Identifying and empathizing with your emotions is the crucial first step of our three-step plan. Here are a few challenges you might face that would cause you to stumble at the very beginning:

- You're too overwhelmed to really think about how you feel: If you're a 10 out of 10 on your emotions elevator, you're probably too heightened to step back and really think about what you're feeling and why it's okay. This might be a good time to update the recipe and calm down both before and after this step. It could look like this: notice overwhelming emotion, take five deep breaths, identify your feelings, and then ground yourself so that those feelings lower even further.

- You lack empathy for yourself: We've been conditioned to not like our anger. How many times have you been told that you shouldn't act the way you do? This might be true—it's never okay to harm yourself or others—but the reactions you have don't mean that the actual emotion underneath them is bad or wrong. It's also important to recognize that your past history impacts your current reality. You may have had several big, bad things happen to you that make you feel the way you do. Don't give up and swear never to try this recipe again—practice self-acceptance and self-love, and know that your best way forward is by honoring your own emotions.

- You pathologize your emotions: If you're treating your emotions as abnormal and unhealthy, you're saying there's something wrong about having them, and that must mean there's something wrong with you. You may not like your feelings, but it doesn't make you wrong or weird for experiencing them. We may also have a tendency to take away our own responsibility when we pathologize our personal emotions. We label ourselves as abnormal, and then that's just what we are, so it's not our fault. We can't fix things if they're irreparably broken, so why even bother? If this happens, take a step back to ask yourself, "Who's in charge of how I feel? Who's in charge of how I react?" The answer, of course, is you.

**Step 2: Calm down.** If you can't calm down, you can't think clearly. Here are some challenges you could face when you're trying to calm down enough to come up with a game plan:

- You're too overwhelmed to calm down: When we're feeling really heightened on our emotions elevator, it can be hard to calm down, and it may even feel pointless. You may need to stack a few coping skills on top of one another to really feel a noticeable impact. It can also help to measure what you're feeling so you don't lose focus. If you're starting at an 8 out of 10 on your anxiety elevator, a deep breath may lower you down just a half point, but that's still an impact.

- You can't figure out your best tool: If you can't figure out your best tool, you may not have enough tools in your toolbox. Outside of using our three-step approach, it's good to practice a myriad of different relaxation strategies, being open to new experiences. Stay on the lookout for healthy relaxation tips from yoga instructors, therapists on social media, or friends. Plan your go-to skill, so that even if you don't know exactly what helps you calm down, you can at least start with one tool and go from there. You could even try just lying on the ground. It may feel weird, but you are literally grounding yourself, connecting with your physical body, and getting a different perspective on the whole situation.

- You're worried about the perception of others: You may be worried about looking silly in front of someone else. First, who cares what other people think about you? Second, even if you do care, do you have to? Third, if you choose to keep caring, remember that people are pretty myopic and self-interested. Few people are paying as much attention to you as you pay to yourself. Finally, what's your list of coping skills you can do that feel less obvious to the outside world? It's hard to really tell when someone is taking deep breaths. If you're squeezing and relaxing your toes in your shoes, who's going to notice? If you rest your eyes a few moments, you can tell your friends you're closing your eyes because you're tired, and you're simultaneously guiding yourself through a calming visualization. Anxiety tends to tell you that *everyone is watching*, because it wants to keep you safe. Your anxiety doesn't always know best.

**Step 3: Come up with a game plan.** Game planning can be the most complex part of this three-step approach, and this is where further training and practice will really benefit you. The more you try different plans in different situations, the more experience you'll have under your belt, and the more data you get for next time. Here are three big challenges that you can face within the game-planning stage:

- You get stuck on finding a "perfect" solution: Let's go back to that crème brûlée. You make a dozen little crème brûlées for a party, and you and your friend, Marcus, try one together. Marcus tells you it's delicious, but you notice that the custard doesn't quite meet your expectations. There's a tiny bit of curdled egg at the bottom, and it seems kind of watery too. Should you throw out the whole batch? If you're stuck on perfect, you probably would, even though that means a ton more work—and you're not even guaranteed a perfect outcome next time. When you're game planning and none of your proposed solutions sound perfect, try to pick a good enough version to get you moving forward, rather than waiting and waiting to figure out a perfect solution.

- You can't move past what happened: When you're really hurt by a problem, it can be difficult to move on with your life. This is okay. Some hurts are too big to move past in the moment. Ask yourself, what part of the problem makes it hard to move on? Are you blaming yourself for any portion of it? Are you feeling shame or guilt? When it's difficult to move past a problem, even if you'd really like to, it may be time to call in an expert. Talking with a therapist or counselor, even a school counselor you trust, can provide a helpful perspective, and can help you figure out how to move forward with your life even when something really difficult or upsetting has happened.

- Your problem isn't actually solvable: Sometimes we can't change what's happening. We're not in charge of everyone and everything. We're only in charge of ourselves. When we're stuck in a problem that can't be solved, we have to figure out a way to accept our circumstances and do our best within those limitations.

Identifying and empathizing, calming down, and game planning provide a framework you can use in any future stressful situation, but remember that you have many tools at your disposal, including reaching out to a local therapist or counselor. Having this recipe doesn't mean that you always need to do it on your own. You probably really value solving everything yourself—but it's good to ask for help too.

# CHAPTER 8

# Change Doesn't Happen Unless You Want It

## (and You're Motivated Enough to Follow Through)

You're on the final chapter of this book, and you've already learned so much. You have! Through your work during this whole book, you've built an invaluable skill set that will help you move forward with your anxiety and anger, without feeling like your anxiety takes over, and without having to regret your angry reactions. Learning about these tools and starting to notice your progress is wonderful, and it also means you still have room to grow. It may take more than one reading to really understand everything in this book, and it takes practice to consistently use these many skills in real life.

Have you wanted to take a break from this book? Have you felt overwhelmed by it? Were there times when you tried out some of these techniques, but they didn't work in the moment so you just decided to give up? Does anything in particular feel too hard to change? If any of your answers are yes, pay attention to that. These questions are important—and the feelings and concerns they bring up are both valid and oh so common.

When things are hard or don't go our way, it can seem very appealing to just give up. We get burned by the times we make an effort and it fails. Part of us wants to just give up fully. It's hard to keep the momentum going when you feel you've met a roadblock.

There's a balance between opting out of the struggle, as we talk about in Chapter 4, and just totally numbing out and disengaging. Numbing out can feel really appealing. You build a protective shell around yourself, and you don't ever leave it. At times you may want to act like a turtle. You'll want to duck inside your shell and take a break, and not have to deal with the outside world at all. Being a turtle can be great! However, you can't turtle up all the time. You still have to get out there. You still have to try.

It takes effort to feel your anxiety and anger. You get to choose to deal with the challenges you face without exploding. Even as you're building up your emotional regulation skills, you may be afraid for yourself in future stressful situations. You've had years of reacting to anxiety triggers explosively. Rewiring your brain doesn't happen overnight.

The way you get through setbacks without feeling totally disheartened is by keeping in mind your capacity for positive change, and by having a mental picture of how things will positively improve if everything works out. Setbacks don't feel quite so insurmountable if you know there's still a path forward and a goal you can reach.

In this chapter, let's talk about setting your goals for managing your anxiety-driven anger, and staying motivated even when you get off track. We're going to identify what situations might feel like big challenges for you, and we're also going to celebrate what you've accomplished already. Let's approach this as your graduation from this book! You can always come back and review anything you need to—but you deserve your imaginary graduation cap and certificate for getting through this whole behemoth.

## WHAT'S YOUR FUTURE?

To say hello to the next stage of life, you have to say good-bye to the stage before. Like when you're graduating from high school and you're leaving behind homerooms and school plays, study halls and winter formals, in order to move forward. Even when it's sad to leave something behind, we're designed to move forward, and we can acknowledge our loss of the past while still feeling excited about what is coming up next.

There may be parts of your former life that you won't miss at all, and parts of it that you will. Finishing this book is going to be the start of a new chapter for you. You will be able to say good-bye to explosive outbursts, at least some of the time. You'll be saying good-bye to not knowing why you're overwhelmed and not knowing what to do with it. You'll also say good-bye, though, to feeling like anger happens only to you, or that problems are never your fault. You won't be able to blame others for all your problems. You won't be able to ignore your rising anxiety or stress levels. You'll have to tune in a lot more to everything. It's going to be different.

But different isn't bad. Different isn't even good. Different just *is*. Your life will be different now that you've finished *When Anxiety Makes You Angry*. You're stepping into a new stage. I believe that, overall, this stage will be great for you. Let's picture it.

## YOUR FUTURE SELF

Things will not always go your way. That's just a fact. When times get tough, you want to have an image or a picture to hold that gets you through the hard stuff. Let's visualize this future together. We'll start by relaxing. Then I'll ask you a few questions, and I want you to just picture your responses inside your mind.

As with every guided visualization we do together, start by finding a comfortable seat, or even lying down on your bed, the couch, or the floor. Take a few slow, deep breaths. Breathe gently in through your nose, pause, and then out through your mouth, and pause. In, pause, out, pause. Notice just a gentle beat between each inhale and exhale. Repeat this paused breathing five times, and then let your breath return to normal.

Check in with the muscles in your forehead, your face, and your neck. If anything feels tight, let it soften.

Move down to the muscles across your shoulders, and let your shoulders soften and relax down your back.

Let your arms get heavy. Feel your fingers and the palms of your hands. Let your hands soften and relax.

Notice your heartbeat. Notice the muscles around your stomach. If your heart feels fast or your abdominal muscles feel tight, just let your calm breath travel down to those areas. Let those areas soften and relax.

Move this spotlight of attention down the fronts and the backs of your legs, softening any tension in your hips and legs if you can.

Finally, check in with your feet, and notice all the way down to the tips of your toes. Let every tiny muscle in your feet relax and soften, supported by gravity.

For a moment, just close your eyes to check in with your whole body. Soften any remaining tightness or stiffness, gently, as much as you can. Feel all your muscles, from your head to your toes, soft and heavy and relaxed.

In this relaxed moment, your mind is more open to new possibilities and able to observe things a little differently. Review these questions, one section at a time, and then close your eyes to really paint a picture of your future. You'll have a chance to write, draw, or make notes about your experience after each view into the future.

**Six months from now:**

Picture yourself six months in the future. Take a step back and observe yourself, just like you were watching a movie on a screen. Think about the goals you may have had for yourself when you began this book.

- If everything worked out the way you want it to, after finishing this book and using the skills you've learned, what does your life look like?

- If you're now more in charge of your anxiety-driven anger, how do you interact with your parents? How does that relationship look and feel to you?

- What are your relationships like with your friends? What do you notice is happening for you, internally, when you are with your friends? How is that different from your present moment?

- Let's say you end up interacting with a teacher at school who would normally drive you crazy. What does that look like six months from now? How do you handle it? What's the same? What's different?

- What would other people notice about you?

- When you face a challenge, one that may have even caused an anxiety spike or an explosive outburst in the past, how do you respond to it now?

- Six months from now, what might you still need help with? What might you still need to work on?

*✱ Take a minute to jot down a few notes, draw a picture, or just type out a memo to yourself on your phone about your vision for six months from now. You may have observed some great things, and you may have identified some areas to continue working on. Thinking about a more ideal version of yourself in six months, what's one step you can take today to get you closer to that goal? Choose a day in your calendar around six months from now to check in with this vision. When you're ready, take another slow breath in through your nose and out through your mouth. Soften your forehead, shoulders, and your breath. Center yourself. ✱*

**One year from now:**

- Think about where you'll be in school. Can you imagine yourself in your next year of school, as a junior or a senior, or new college student?

- Picture yourself walking through the halls of your school. How do you interact with your classmates as you pass them? Your teachers?

- What academic choices have you made to get you to this point?

- How did you handle the increase in responsibility when it came time to select your classes, build your schedule, and decide what was most important to you?

- Picture yourself at home, one year from now, either living at home or visiting from college. What are your interactions like with your parents? With any siblings? Do you like what you see?

- One year from now, there's excitement, but also new challenges. How do you manage the pros and the cons in this new year?

- Let's say all your goals for yourself, after reading this book, have come to fruition. How does that look externally? How does that feel internally?

- How do you act toward others? What's your relationship like with yourself?

- When you observe your future self, how do you feel right now, in this moment? You may feel anxious, but anxiety and excitement often go hand in hand. Focus on your excitement, eagerness, or even just a sense of calm that comes up for you as you observe your future self. Feel that feeling in your heart.

*✳ Try to be as observant as possible during this visualization. What do you want to keep with you and remember? What details are the most important? What feelings do you want to hold on to that you experienced during this visualization? How realistic is this? What's one particular step you can take today to get closer to this goal? ✳*

Teens with anxiety often get caught up in what-ifs, like, "What if this terrible thing happens?" or "What if so-and-so is mad at me?" "What if I get a bad grade on this test?" or "What if I lose?" or "What if my life stinks forever?"

There's a flip side when it comes to what-if-ing yourself. What if everything works out? What if everything is great? What if that thing you thought would be tough is easy, that math test is a breeze, that friend drama is quickly forgotten and moved past? Our brain is naturally primed to think about worst-case scenarios, so it's helpful to instead think through best-case scenarios. None of us can see into the future. Something bad could happen, but something awesome could happen too.

That's part of this guided visualization activity. Anxious minds can catastrophize way into the future, like how our anxiety spirals start with one small worry and turn into this huge, life-ruining premonition. Positively visualizing your future self is flipping the script. What if everything works out? What if you meet your goals? What if you take all these skills you've learned from this book and apply them more often than not?

Guided visualizations are pretty cool, because you are the person coming up with that image. Your brain is doing all the work by answering the prompts and taking those words to create a detailed picture in your head, linking to your emotions and your physical experience in the moment. Your brain is a hugely powerful tool.

When you picture your ideal future self, you can increase your level of relaxation and optimism and your general sense of wellness. This increase is a goal. Hopefully, it's an attainable goal for you, even when there are stumbling blocks. When you start to drift too far off the path toward this future self, or when you start to feel too challenged to continue working on managing your anxiety and anger, come back to this picture. Remind yourself. Reassess and readdress what you need to. Get realigned with your goals.

You may have heard this trite saying before: "If you believe it, you can achieve it." Now, to be frank, that's not always true. I could believe that I'll become a unicorn one day, and even have vivid dreams about becoming a unicorn, but that's not actually going to happen. Some things are just beyond our reach. However, it does speak to an important point: when you have goals that are achievable, your motivation goes a long way in helping you to achieve them.

## SETTING GOALS

To make your goals more reachable, like those goals you saw for your future self, you need to break them down into pieces, check in regularly, and focus on your sphere of influence. SMART goals, a term first coined by authors George Doran, Arthur Miller, and James Cunningham, is an acronym that guides you into creating doable goals (1981). You may have seen (or perhaps will see) this acronym using slightly different wording, but here's the best way, I think, to break it down.

## Specific

It's great to have a goal like, "I want to be successful in my future," but what does that goal really mean? How do you measure success? How far in the future do you want this to happen? Drill down a little into what this goal means, in order to make it more specific. For you, being successful might mean having a certain career. For others, being successful might mean having the financial freedom to travel the world without ever having to work. Maybe the biggest goal you have right now, when you sit with it, is being successful at managing your anxiety-driven anger. We'll use this as our goal for each part of the acronym.

**Goal:** *I want to stop having anxious outbursts that get in the way of my life.*

## Measurable

You should be able to track your progress on your goals. Tracking helps you stay motivated, because you know when you're improving, and you also know when you need to readjust. For example, you may have a goal to do better in school. Again, this is a wonderful goal, but how would you measure it? Is it going to come down to your GPA? Or is it more of an issue of actually completing assignments on time instead of getting caught up in perfectionism to the point where nothing is good enough to turn in? To track this goal, you want to have measurable benchmarks. First, you'll see how many assignments out of ten you're turning in on time during a typical week as your base level, and you'll measure up from there. Maybe your first step would be turning in six out of ten assignments, then eight out of ten, then ten out of ten. "Do better at school" isn't measurable if you don't have a set data point you're tracking.

**Goal:** *I want to stop having anxious outbursts that get in the way of my life. I'll track my anxiety level on an emotions elevator, and mark down how many days*

*I reach a 10 out of 10, then work on keeping the total number of 10 out of 10 days lower each month.*

## Achievable

Goals should be within your grasp, not something that's impossible to reach. Figure out how you'd be able to tell that you've reached your goal, and what it would look like if you didn't. "I want to go to a good college" is a fine goal, and doable depending on your grades and the admissions process. But what does a "good college" look like to you? Is it a college that is super elite and only lets in 2 percent of applicants? Or is a good college one where you can take the classes you want and still get a good GPA? Maybe the state college is a good college for you, because you'll get in, and you'll have access to many more classes than you would at a small, private school.

**Goal:** *I want to stop having anxious outbursts that get in the way of my life. I'll track my anxiety level on an emotions elevator, mark down how many days I reach a 10 out of 10, then work on reaching a 10 out of 10 only one day per month maximum.*

## Realistic and Relevant

Along with being achievable, you want your goals to be both realistic and relevant. Your goal should be something that you can reach, and it should also align with the other goals you have for yourself, to help you stay motivated. "I want to travel to Mars as an astronaut" and "I want to make the best ever double chocolate cookie" aren't really relevant to one another. "I want to become a professional chef" and "I want to perfect my double chocolate cookie recipe" tie in a little better. That's not to say that you can't have many different interests in your life, but our minds have a tendency to focus on shiny objects, always looking for the next totally cool, different thing. Try to keep your goals a little closer together.

> **Goal:** *I want to stop having anxious outbursts that get in the way of my life. I'll track my anxiety level on an emotions elevator, mark down how many days I reach a 10 out of 10, then work on reaching a 10 out of 10 only one day per month maximum. (Right now, I reach a 10 out of 10 at least twice a day, so I know this goal will take some time, but this is probably doable.)*

## Time-Sensitive

Goals have a way of filling up as much time as you give them. Because your goal will already be specific, measurable, attainable, and realistic/relevant, you'll know precisely what you're looking for, and you'll know how to measure it. Set a deadline, break your goal into smaller steps, and check in regularly. If you want to fight with your parents less, you'll need to check in regularly instead of just having this goal in the back of your mind. So, you'd see how much you're fighting now, and you'd try to curb the number of arguments you have with them within the next two weeks. Then, you'd try to lower that even more and add in relaxation skills when it seems like a fight is about to start. Maybe your goal is to fight only once a month maximum by the time you graduate.

> **Goal:** *I want to stop having anxious outbursts that get in the way of my life. I'll track my anxiety level on an emotions elevator, mark down how many days I reach a 10 out of 10, then work on reaching a 10 out of 10 only one day per month maximum. (Right now, I reach a 10 out of 10 at least twice a day, so I know this goal will take some time, but this is probably doable.) I'll track that emotions elevator in the morning, and jot down the days that I meditate. Next month, I'll graph all my elevators to see if that anxiety is trending downward and assess how many days I listened to a meditation. Based on the data, I'll make changes to this plan, and assess again in another month.*

## COMING BACK TO THE IDEAL

When you have a vision of yourself that you'd like to achieve, it can feel disheartening if you get off track. You'd like to be a calmer person who is less prone to anxious, angry outbursts, but if you find yourself fighting with parents and friends more and more, it can almost seem impossible to reach that goal.

Remember that you will get off track. There's never a straight shot. Goals don't just happen—they have to be worked on regularly, and that's true for everyone.

Picture a recent college graduate, Sam, who is feeling pretty lost. Her life always fulfilled her own and her parents' wishes. She always received good grades and went from elementary school to a prestigious private middle and high school. She got into her top-choice college. And now she's graduated and doesn't know what to do next. Sam wanted to be a journalist and applied for a few internships, but wasn't accepted into any of them. She was so focused on reaching each step of her planned trajectory that she hadn't really thought about what would happen if she didn't make it to the next step right away. It was like running down a set of stairs and then realizing that, suddenly, you've missed a step. You feel a lurch in your stomach. Your progress is immediately stopped because you have to totally reassess.

When you feel totally off course, remember that you're not. You might be driving a go-cart off the track onto the grass, but you're still moving.

Sam is so shaken by not getting an internship, and not having a clear path to go forward, that she decides to go to counseling. When talking with her therapist, Sam explains that she has started to retreat from her friends, fight with her parents, and close in on herself. In order to feel better, Sam needs to remember that she is good enough, even when she thinks her life is on pause.

# THE "GOOD ENOUGH" CLAUSE

It's helpful to keep your ideal vision of yourself in your head as an image to come back to when you're feeling low, disheartened, or unmotivated. Sam had an ideal in her head of what she wanted to be when she "grew up," but then her immediate postcollege reality didn't match up to this goal.

Rather than totally throwing this vision and goal away, though, to focus on the here and now, Sam can create a "good enough" clause. Yes, Sam wants to keep her ideal in mind, and at the same time, she can create a "good enough" version of events given her current reality, then aim to get closer to that version while still keeping the big journalism goal in mind.

The good-enough clause gives you an out when you're not matching up with your ideal. In terms of your anger management work, your ideal may be to never fight with your best friend again. That would be wonderful! No more fights with your buddy! But then, what happens the next time you two get into an argument? You feel totally disheartened and miserable. Not only are you fighting, but you're also letting yourself down. In this type of situation, you want to ask yourself, what's the good enough version of your goal for now? Maybe it's too hard to totally stop fighting, but what if a good enough goal is to stop fighting about where to go grab food, or to stop using insults when you fight, or to stop and take a deep breath whenever you feel that urge to argue?

Maybe your goal is to never have another panic attack in school. That would also feel amazing—and it could even be realistic! The next time you have a panic attack in school, though, you might be tempted to give up. Instead, think through your good-enough clause. What's a good enough version of this goal, for right now and in this moment? Maybe it's good enough to keep it to one panic attack a week? Maybe it's good enough to keep your panic attacks to under five minutes, or to be able to rejoin class right after instead of needing to take a break in the nurse's office? Maybe it's good enough to try three coping skills every time you have a panic attack, even if it doesn't stop your anxiety from spiking?

Sam's good-enough clause could focus on still enjoying writing. While her goal of becoming a journalist is far out of reach at this time, and not getting an internship right out of school makes her feel hopeless, the good-enough clause would help her stay motivated even during disappointments. Even though she isn't working as an intern, she could still write and even research how to submit pieces to different publications. She could still go on informational interviews. She could still reach out to her alumni network and email connections.

Sam can still live her life and recognize that the disappointment she felt was valid, but it wasn't everything she had going on. She still has her friends and her family. She could get a job at a fun restaurant in town and become buddies with her coworkers. She could go on dates. She could investigate topics that interest her and write essays for herself, continuing to work on her craft. And she could stay in therapy to explore all the feelings that were coming up after missing the next step she thought she would reach right away.

As you think of your goals, remember that good enough can be good enough. You can still work toward your ideal while being okay with the present and finding ways to work within a set of constraints you don't love. Your good-enough clause allows you to be satisfied in the moment, recognizing that a small step is still a step in the right direction.

## WHAT HAVE YOU ALREADY LEARNED?

Let's review all the skills you've from learned this book, related to problems you might face in the future and keyed to the relevant chapters. This way, you'll be able to easily reference anything you need. We'll also talk about how to "level up" your skills, building on your foundation and taking the skills even further.

Feel free to create your own list in your phone or on a sheet of paper you can keep in this book (if you own it!) and organize based on additional problems you might face yourself.

## How do I deal with annoying parents?

Parents can be totally annoying! Even when they don't mean to be.

- If you're not sure what you're feeling about them, check out the body scan drawings in Chapter 1.

  *Level Up:* Journal about the emotions coming up for you, and how those feelings are impacting your thoughts and behaviors around your parents.

- If you need some coping skills to make sure you don't explode when they're annoying you, practice the skills laid out in Chapter 5.

  *Level Up:* Search online for guided meditations.

- Is there a particular problem you need to solve? You always have a choice to work things out or just move on. If there is something that you think you can solve or compromise on, use SILLY to walk you through your steps.

  *Level Up:* Set aside a calm time to discuss this problem with your parents (if you think this will be a constructive conversation—if not, it might be time to search for a family therapist). Get their input on how they think you've been handling conflict with them. Take their feedback and modify your problem-solving options. And set up a time to regularly check in with them on a biweekly basis.

## What should I do when I get too angry?

What's clueing you into the fact that you're "too" angry? Remember that it's okay to feel anger. It's a healthy emotion.

- Review your anger iceberg in Chapter 1 and explore what emotions are coming up for you underneath the surface of this anger.

  *Level Up:* Practice acceptance of all the emotions underneath the surface, not just anger. Review Chapter 3 too!

- Walk through your most recent time of feeling "too angry" and chart it on your window of tolerance (Chapter 4).

  *Level Up:* Start recording your window of tolerance right after you've experienced an upsetting event and keep these records together to start noticing trends.

- As always, coping skills are key to managing overwhelming emotions. Review all the coping skills in Chapter 5 and see how we apply them in our three-step approach walk-throughs in Chapter 7.

  *Level Up:* Using coping skills on your own only get you so far. It might be time to find a counselor in your area, just so you have someone to talk to about your anger and underlying emotions. If it's too big to handle on your own, it's always okay to seek out additional help from a trained professional.

## How can I handle an overwhelming breakup?

Breakups can really stink, even when they're ultimately for the best. No matter if you're on the breaking-up or broken-up-with side, there's helpful information available for you:

- Consider the cognitive triangle (Chapter 2) and use this framework to identify your thoughts, feelings, and behaviors around the breakup.

  *Level Up:* In addition to identifying thoughts, feelings, and behaviors, notice whether you're having an anxiety spiral (Chapter 6), and write it down so that you can get a more clear-eyed view of what's going on for you cognitively.

- Review your restructuring, acceptance, and hybrid option about your thoughts in Chapter 6. Remember that you can choose to really dig in and come up with something more helpful to tell yourself, but it's also a great choice to just recognize that these thoughts are normal and natural, and that it makes a lot of sense that they would come up.

  *Level Up:* Whatever route you choose, create a reminder for yourself somewhere that you'll regularly see it. You could write down your statement of acceptance on a Post-it and stick it on your desk. You could write a reminder to yourself on your phone about a more helpful thought. You could create an art project that represents your mind feeling more at ease, and hang it up. Figure out what's impactful for you and put it somewhere you can see it.

- Anxious minds tend to get a little obsessed after something upsetting like a breakup. If you're noticing thoughts come up all the time about this breakup, use the paper boats guided meditation in Chapter 5.

  *Level Up:* Different people respond to different metaphors: clouds, leaves, boats, the ocean, and so on. Try out several versions and find what's most impactful for your mind.

## Feeling worried about college?

College is such an exciting time of your life, and such a big step toward independent adulthood, that it makes sense to feel worried about it. There are lots of aspects to think about, like what college is best, what you should major in, or how to get the most out of your college experience. These questions can't all be answered in a bulleted list, so the Level Up suggestions are particularly important under this heading.

- Consider what you are in charge of, and what you're not in charge of. For example, you're in charge of your application materials, sending in the submissions, and collecting the letters of reference. You're not in charge of whether the college lets you in. Think about what else you want to add to this list from Chapter 6.

  *Level Up:* Keep your sphere of influence in mind. While you're not in charge of getting into colleges, you are able to influence their decision by the choices you make. What experiences would help enrich you and make you more desirable to colleges? What courses could you take that interest you while also making you appealing to the admissions board? How can you influence the community around you through volunteerism and acts of service that feel fulfilling to you and also tick off an important box? Working for the benefit of the greater good also benefits you individually.

- You don't have to have everything figured out about college before you get there, but it is helpful to think about what you would like to feel like. Go through the future-self exercise here in Chapter 8, applying it to college specifically.

  *Level Up:* Another tool to try is the perfect-day exercise. Here's a condensed version: Imagine you're waking up in college on your perfect day. Add all the details about what you're doing, where you're going, and how you're feeling. Figure out one or two changes you can make to get you closer to this ideal. Keep this perfect day in mind as you apply to colleges, and also when you actually get there.

- Are you worried about managing your anxiety-driven anger when you're all alone at college? What if you explode in front of everyone? What if your anxiety gets too overwhelming to finish up assignments or take tests? Remember that you're building your coping skills toolbox (Chapter 5), and that you've got your three-step approach for managing overwhelming situations (Chapter 7).

  *Level Up:* If this fear is coming up for you, remember that counseling is always an option. You can work with someone on college readiness, so that you feel more prepared before you get there. Colleges also have counseling departments, and you can seek out therapy once you're there. I recommend starting therapy at least the summer before you go off to college, so that you have built up a relationship with your therapist, and addressed your concerns, and you have a support person in place before you head off to campus.

## DO I NEED COUNSELING?

This is a great, important question, and it's a question that comes down to you. While this book can offer some ideas to consider, the best way to know is to complete an assessment with a licensed mental health therapist.

Counseling or therapy (two terms often used interchangeably, along with psychotherapy) can be a hugely important tool for improving your mental health. Deciding to start therapy is a decision you'll make for yourself (along with, depending on your age, your parents). Here are a few things to keep in mind as you're making this decision:

- You need to find a therapist who is a great fit for you, because that's often the biggest predictor of success in counseling. Think about your favorite teachers, coaches, and other helpful adults in your life. What qualities do they have in common? What makes them feel helpful? These are the traits you want to look for in a therapist.

- What are your goals for therapy? What do you want to leave with? Your therapist may help you discover more things to work on beyond this original plan, but it's good to keep in mind what you want to work on and why.

- Think, too, about what being successful in therapy would look like to you. Does it mean fewer outbursts? A better understanding of yourself? More coping skills? Just feeling like you have space to vent and an empathetic listener? There are tons of different types of therapy approaches out there, and you get to decide if you want to be more skills oriented or more focused on just processing what's going on in your life.

If you decide that you do want to get therapy, and you have thought about the questions above, what do you do next? How do you even start?

- If you're under eighteen (or in some states, under sixteen, and in the state of Washington, under thirteen, so check around to find your state's laws), you'll need your parents' permission, and their signatures, on your consent forms. Talk to them about why you think counseling would be helpful. Counseling is a potential solution to your problems—so, remember SILLY. You're staying calm and you've already investigated the problem. Let your parents know why you want it, listen to their feedback, and figure out if it's a yes or a no. If, for some reason, their answer is no, you can still consider counseling at your school.

- Once you've advocated for your mental health needs and your parents are on board, search for local counselors in your area. Nowadays, it's easy to find therapists online. A quick way to pull up some good names is to search for "anxiety counseling near me," and see what therapists' websites pop up. There are also therapist directories, and there are certainly going to be nonprofits that offer mental health counseling— at least in the nearest big city, if not right in your town. If you're comfortable with it, ask your friends for recommendations. Check out a few therapists's profiles and see who you think you'd click with.

- After you've narrowed down your list, you and/or your parents should reach out to a couple of counselors and set up a quick phone consult, just to talk through their approach and make sure they seem like a good fit for you. Remember, the biggest predictor of a good outcome from therapy is your relationship with your therapist. While it can take time to build up a relationship, and you should give yourself at least a few sessions before you decide whether they're the right therapist for you, it's great to start from a place of feeling like you could get along with this person and that they could help you.

## CONGRATULATIONS!

Alright, alright, I told you in Chapter 5 that I would only use an exclamation point in a subheading once, but I think I'm allowed one more. It's a celebration, after all!

You've made it through this whole book. You've finished *When Anxiety Makes You Angry*! Now what?

Hopefully, you have many takeaways from this book: lessons you've absorbed, skills you've built, and realizations you want to keep with you. So how are you going to move forward with this knowledge? It's up to you.

Picture yourself, standing about a quarter of the way up on a huge mountain. You've already come so far—but you have so much farther to go. There are rocks and a dusty path winding out in front of you. It doesn't look like easy going, but you get to decide what to do. You can sit and take a pause and catch your breath. You might decide to change your shoes. You might run up the mountain or walk really slowly and carefully. You might even decide to go on a different trail that meanders off to the side but looks beautiful. You can hop, skip, jump, or crawl—you are fully in charge of how you travel forward.

You are climbing your own mountain in life. You will face boulders and steep inclines, and you'll also find easy, flat parts on the trail, and beautiful scenery to admire. Nobody else will be on this mountain with you. You might have parents or teachers, or even friends, try to dictate how you should climb your mountain, but it's not up to them. You might have coaches or therapists or books (like this one) giving you tips on ways to be a better mountaineer, but it's not up to them how you climb your mountain—it is fully up to you. You are making your own way.

No matter what happens, and no matter how hard it feels, I believe in your ability to face what's coming.

Even if you look way ahead on the path and see some steep cliffs, know that you have the skills to get past them and that you can get help when you need it. Even if you decide you need a moment to just rest, know that you know yourself best, and that you know what you need better than anyone. You will make your own way forward in whatever way you need to.

You've got this.

# Acknowledgments

There are many people I'd like to pass my gratitude along to, and this is just a partial list. Many thanks to the following:

To my husband, Kyle, who doesn't much go for public displays of affection. I'll keep it brief: I couldn't have written this book without you.

To my social worker mother, who made me who I am and walked with me through this book-writing, therapizing process.

To my father, who showed me how to be social and bright and kind and funny. You help me take myself less seriously.

To Emileigh Barnes, my college roommate and genius friend, who read through and helped me craft my whole pitch. I don't think this book would've gotten made without you.

So much gratitude goes out to the staff at Compassionate Counseling St. Louis, especially to Lauren Goldberger, my intake coordinator, who helped me whenever I had a research request or wanted to pick her brain on how best to write this book for the people who really need it.

Mallory Grimste, Rachel Baker, and Nikki Sewell, I am so lucky to have you as fellow businesswomen. Your support (and space for venting) has meant the world.

I'd also like to express my heartfelt gratitude to Miranda Palmer, my business coach, who reminded me how important it was to take the time for this book and to recognize that there is a balance between being a new mom, a business owner, and an author. Whenever I fell off the path toward finishing this book, you gently guided me back on.

I wouldn't have been able to write this book without my clients. Thank you to the many kids, teens, college students, and families who have trusted me over the years; who have been willing to dig in, do the work, and listen to someone who tells them, "You're not angry, you're anxious." You have all inspired me.

And finally, thank you very much to the whole team at New Harbinger, and especially to Tesilya Hanauer for helping me craft the idea for this book; Jennye Garibaldi and Caleb Beckwith for the edits; my copyeditor Karen Schader, who got me to the point a whole lot quicker; and the whole marketing team. I feel so lucky that you believed in me and this work.

# Resources

The following worksheets and tools, referenced within this book, can be downloaded at www.kelseytorgersondunn.com.

1. Guide for Parents

2. The Anger Iceberg

3. The Body Clues Outline

4. CBT Triangles Worksheet

5. Thought Spirals Worksheet

6. The Window of Tolerance

7. The Perfect Day Guided Visualization

8. Relaxation Walkthroughs

# References

Doran, G. T. 1981. "There's a S.M.A.R.T. Way to Write Management's Objectives." *Management Review* 70 (11): 35–36.

Månsson, K., A. Salami, A. Frick, et al. 2016. "Neuroplasticity in Response to Cognitive Behavior Therapy for Social Anxiety Disorder." *Transl Psychiatry* 6, e727. https://doi.org/10.1038/tp.2015.218

Ogden, P., K. Minton, and C. Pain. 2006. *Trauma and the Body: A Sensorimotor Approach to Psychotherapy*. New York: W. W. Norton & Company.

Siegel, D. J. 2012. *The Developing Mind: How Relationships and the Brain Interact to Shape Who We Are*. New York: Guilford Press.

**Kelsey Torgerson Dunn, MSW, LCSW,** specializes in anxiety and anger management therapy for kids, teens, and college students. She opened her group practice, Compassionate Counseling St. Louis, in early 2017. She practices cognitive behavioral therapy (CBT), acceptance and commitment therapy (ACT), and mindfulness skills, and often finds that just having someone on your side is the most helpful part of counseling.

Foreword writer **Mallory Grimste, LCSW,** is an adolescent mental health specialist with a counseling practice in Woodbridge, CT. To maximize her impact in helping teens improve their mental health, she shares new videos every week and offers a variety of guided self-help resources and programs on her website, www.mallorygrimste.com.

# More ⏱Instant Help Books for Teens

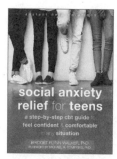

### SOCIAL ANXIETY RELIEF FOR TEENS

A Step-by-Step CBT Guide to Feel Confident and Comfortable in Any Situation

**978-1684037056 / US $16.95**

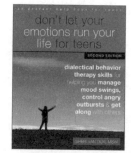

### DON'T LET YOUR EMOTIONS RUN YOUR LIFE FOR TEENS, SECOND EDITION

Dialectical Behavior Therapy Skills for Helping You Manage Mood Swings, Control Angry Outbursts, and Get Along with Others

**978-1684037360 / US $18.95**

### THE RESILIENT TEEN

10 Key Skills to Bounce Back from Setbacks and Turn Stress into Success

**978-1684035786 / US $17.95**

### THE ANGER WORKBOOK FOR TEENS, SECOND EDITION

Activities to Help You Deal with Anger and Frustration

**978-168403245- / US $17.95**

### CONQUER NEGATIVE THINKING FOR TEENS

A Workbook to Break the Nine Thought Habits That Are Holding You Back

**978-1626258891 / US $17.95**

### THE GROWTH MINDSET WORKBOOK FOR TEENS

Say Yes to Challenges, Deal with Difficult Emotions, and Reach Your Full Potential

**978-1684035571 / US $18.95**

🌱 **newharbinger**publications

1-800-748-6273 / newharbinger.com

(VISA, MC, AMEX / prices subject to change without notice)     Follow Us 📷📘🐦▶📌📷🔗

Sign up for book alerts! **Go to newharbinger.com/bookalerts** ✨

# Did you know there are **free tools** you can download for this book?

Free tools are things like **worksheets**, **guided meditation exercises**, and **more** that will help you get the most out of your book.

You can download free tools for this book— whether you bought or borrowed it, in any format, from any source—from the New Harbinger website. All you need is a NewHarbinger.com account. Just use the URL provided in this book to view the free tools that are available for it. Then, click on the "download" button for the free tool you want, and follow the prompts that appear to log in to your NewHarbinger.com account and download the material.

You can also save the free tools for this book to your **Free Tools Library** so you can access them again anytime, just by logging in to your account! Just look for this button on the book's free tools page.

**+ Save this to my free tools library**